EASY THE HARD WAY

EASY
THE HARD WAY

by Joe Pasternak

AS TOLD TO DAVID CHANDLER

Illustrated

G. P. Putnam's Sons, New York

© *1956 by Joe Pasternak*

Library of Congress Catalog Card
Number: 56-6624

MANUFACTURED IN THE UNITED STATES OF AMERICA

VAN REES PRESS • NEW YORK

To
Michael, Jeffrey, and Peter,
who one day might like to know how it was;
to Dorothy,
at the very heart of it;
and to my adopted country,
which took in a stranger and made it all possible.

Contents

Contents

EASY THE HARD WAY

1. A Guy Named Joe

OCCASIONALLY, when I'm not too tired after a day on the set, I dream of a huge volume called the Book of Fate. It is like the big old leather book the apothecary used to have in the little town in Hungary where I was born. I remember he used to refer to it, his nose right against the page, whenever one of the town doctors prescribed something he wasn't sure about. The apothecary always seemed amazed by what he found in the book. "Imagine that! Imagine that!" he would say and, as though against his better judgment, he would go ahead and compound the medicine.

So now I dream I find my name in this Book of Fate and learn to my surprise that I have no business whatsoever being where I am today and doing what I'm doing. I dream that it is all someone's stupid clerical error that I spent the day on a sound stage in Culver City, California, or behind a desk fitting together all the elements and temperaments that go into making a motion picture.

I dream that someone keeps shouting, "No, he isn't supposed to be a producer. He's supposed to be a *shammas*. Or is it a Wagnerian tenor? No—that's ridiculous! Someone's got this Book all mixed up." Sometimes he just says, "Imagine that! Imagine that!" just like the old apothecary.

The effect of this is not to startle me into waking. On the contrary, it's such an old dream that I don't mind it at all. There must be some explanation of how and why but I leave it to better and shrewder brains than mine.

I know I broke all the rules. When people took me for a sucker and an easy mark—and a lot of them still do—I didn't mind at all. Once, when I was head of motion picture production in Europe for Universal, I had a chauffeur who worked me on a commission basis. He would telephone various friends of mine who wanted to borrow money from me and tell them where he had driven me that evening and whether I was in the mood or not for a fast touch, and if so, for how much.

"He's at the Ritz," he'd say, "and he's feeling fine. His last two pictures are cleaning up and the boss cabled to say he's doing a great job. He'd go for a hundred easy."

Or he'd warn them off. "The last picture grosses just came in. It's dying. He got a letter today from Laemmle that aged him ten years. Lay off."

For this service, the chauffeur got a flat ten per cent of the gross of anything borrowed from me.

When I heard about it, all my friends thought I ought to fire the man. I gave him a raise. My friends thought I was crazy. Why would I do a thing like that? "I'll tell you," I said. "He kept the pests away when I didn't want to see them and he brought them around when helping a pal made me feel good. Do you think a man like that doesn't deserve a raise?"

So I wasn't smart. When I wanted to leave Universal,

after I came back to this country and made all those pictures with Deanna Durbin, I ran into Louis B. Mayer, then
studio chief at Metro-Goldwyn-Mayer, and one of a number of prospective employers of my soon-to-be-unemployed
talents. He challenged me to a game of pinochle.

Frank Orsatti, our host, took me aside and whispered:
"You're in, Joe. Just play a good game but make him look
even better."

I tried my level best to follow Frank's advice but every
game we played made me look smarter than my opponent.
Try as I would, I couldn't lose. Cards will do that to you.
Mayer, who was innocent of all this huggermugger going
on around him, was amiable when he paid up at the end of
the evening and said goodnight. Orsatti, once we were
alone, jutted a forefinger in my direction.

"What's the matter with you?" he said. "What's the idea
trimming a man you'd like to work for?"

Well, I don't know. From what I have observed of how
to win friends and influence influential people in Hollywood, I would certainly say that my procedure was hazard-
ous. But in my case maybe it wasn't. I know this. I left
Universal on a Friday and set up shop at M-G-M the following Monday.

I've always had fun making pictures. They make plenty
of jokes about ulcers in Hollywood. Too many nice people
I've known there have died too young. Maybe the trouble
is they didn't have fun at their work. I've made it a rule
never to touch anything unless it amuses me, interests me,
one way or the other. I got a chuckle once out of the notion
of having José Iturbi play a boogie-woogie piano in a
picture I made.

"Good heavens," one of my friends said, "how can you even suggest such a thing to him! You don't know what snobs these concert people are. They jump on him hard enough as it is for acting in your pictures."

So I called José, sat him in a chair in my office and approached him undiplomatically. "I'm doing this picture, *As Thousands Cheer,* and there's a sequence at a camp show and one of the soldiers hollers for you to play some boogie-woogie like Meade Lux Lewis. Will you do it?"

"Why not?" José said.

I had fun, too, when I saw Lauritz Melchior at a party standing next to his charming wife, Kleinschen. Lauritz is a mountain of a man, a true German *Heldentenor,* though he's really Danish. I had an actress named Jane Powell, just as tiny and charming as Kleinschen and I thought Lauritz and my little actress would be cute together. You get the idea. They were, too.

Every so often someone gets me in a corner and tries to persuade me to make a social document. I have no objection to such pictures. Lots of them are good. Some even gross a fair amount. But they just aren't for me, that's all.

In Germany, years ago, they wanted me to buy *Maedchen in Uniform.* I didn't even know what it was about. I was younger then, it's true, but I still don't think I'd buy it if I could. My idea of a good story, or a good picture, is one that leaves you feeling a lift afterward. You come out saying to yourself, well, the world isn't such a bad place after all.

Some people say it's a bad world, it's a dangerous world. Everybody in Hollywood has those Steig cartoon ashtrays

6

with a man hiding in a box. The caption reads "People are no damn good." Perhaps it's true but you can't prove it by me.

I was an immigrant, I was a busboy, and inside of eight years I was sent back to Europe to be in charge of a million-dollar operation. Ever since then I'm frank to say there has been a warm spot in my heart for the fairy tale. I believe in people. I like them. About all they've ever cost me was money and if they've had a good story, it was worth the few dollars they got out of me. In other words, they made it a pleasure to give.

One of my Hungarian friends came to me the other day and wanted twenty dollars. This was a small amount of money for him so I asked why.

"Joe," he explained, "I've just met the most beautiful, the most fabulous girl you can imagine. She is witty, she is built like this, she has a face like that—I've been trying to date her for a week. She said she'd go out with me tonight and I've made reservations all over town. Dinner at Larue's—I've ordered it in advance. Then we'll go dancing at Mocambo and over to Ciro's to catch the late show."

"All this for twenty bucks?" I asked incredulously.

"Oh, I can sign the check at these places," he explained. "But I've got to have a twenty for the tips."

So the fairy tale, the happy-ending story, comes naturally to me. I was born as poor as anyone I know, but that's not enough reason for me to pull a long face when I go to work. Maybe, if the Book of Fate had left me where I logically belong, which is to say, a grocer or a small merchant in what is now Romania, or even if I had become a man of some consequence in my native country,

I might feel the urge to tell what a harsh, bitter world this is.

But it hasn't been that way to me. "I've finally figured you out," the late Robert Benchley once said to me. "All you're doing in your pictures is telling the story of your own life. At the crucial moment, the great man, Stokowski, or someone like that, nods his head. Deanna gets her wish, the orchestra is saved, everyone is happy and can go home and get a good night's sleep. And this is because it's always happened to you."

Bob was right. So here's a warning. This is a happy story, with a happy ending.

2. "Listen to the Music"

In our town the postman was easily the most popular man. Children chased after him as he made his rounds. People smiled at him when he passed, as if they hoped that he would reward them with a letter. I alone grew to dread his comings and goings. He reached our house about nine o'clock in the morning. I always tried to arrange it so I would not be there when he came.

I had nothing against the man. It was my Uncle Geza who was the real cause of it all. Uncle Geza had gone to America a few years before, in 1907 to be exact. He had hardly settled down in the new world before his letters began to be filled with what we knew to be the most obvious tall tales, not to say downright lies. Uncle Geza was that kind anyway. In our family he was considered something of a sporting character. He lived in Budapest whereas we lived in a little town in Transylvania. My mother— Uncle Geza's sister—was a strict woman; we children overheard fascinating rumors about Uncle Geza and the many girls who had fallen in love with him, of how he gambled and spent his evenings listening to gypsy music in dimly lit cafés. This was before he went to America, of course.

9

Naturally none of us believed the fantastic stories he sent back. He wrote that it was nothing for every family to have a bathtub of its own. He wrote that the police didn't bother anyone unless he caused trouble. Uncle Geza said if someone didn't like his job, he could just leave it. In the six years he'd been in America, he'd changed his job three times. Once he'd told the owner of the factory that he wished a plague would overtake him, and there was nothing the owner could do about it. He said he had moved from New York to Philadelphia without asking anyone's permission and that he did not even have to report to the police. It was obvious that he regarded us all as ignorant country cousins prepared to believe anything.

Uncle Geza wanted my father to come to America. He said that, among other things, in America he could read newspapers of every political complexion and he was convinced there was going to be trouble in Europe. It was his idea that my father ought to come to the United States, find a job, and one by one, as hundreds of thousands of immigrants were doing, send for his family.

It was easier said than done. My father was the *shammas,* or sexton, of a little synagogue in a town called Szilagy-Somlyo. We were about 7,500 in that town, with the population evenly divided among Catholics, Protestants, and Jews. It was a beautiful town, set among green mountains, with a cool, wide stream running through the valley. My father was an important man in that town. He opened the little synagogue every morning and closed it at night; he saw to all the details of marriages and deaths and *brisses,* or ritual circumcisions. He was a tall man, with clear blue eyes and reddish hair. He had a long, virile beard and a gentle manner. I never heard my father say a harsh word about anybody and I am sure a harsh thought never entered his head.

The idea of war, which his brother-in-law wrote about from America, did not disturb him too much. He believed people were good; sometimes they were misled, but no one, in his view, would set the world on fire out of malice or wickedness. As for his going to America, it wasn't only that the congregation depended on him. His own mother still lived in the old country and he had been brought up to respect the ancient virtues of filial love. He could not leave his family.

He wrote this to Uncle Geza, and Uncle Geza, always the clever one, answered that perhaps may father might start the ball rolling by sending over one of his children. My father replied that he loved all his children equally and he could not bear the thought of losing any one of them. He had eight children at this time; still he was that kind of man.

Anyway, every time the postman delivered a letter from Uncle Geza I knew it spelled trouble. That's why I tried to arrange matters so that I wouldn't be around when the mail was delivered.

One day, however, the postman found me in the town market. "You'd better go home," he said. "Your father wants to see you."

I had a job in the market. You might say that I had become the composer of the first singing commercials. The tradesmen used to hire youngsters to stand before their shops to yell the high quality of the merchandise

11

inside. I improved on it by setting the whole business to music. I had only to go to the market and the merchants would begin to bid among themselves for my services. I could make a singing commercial about one man's pots and pans or another's beans that made them all seek me out. I made as much being a huckster as my father did serving God. It wasn't much, but when you're twelve years old it doesn't take much to make you feel important.

Anyway, when the postman told me to go home, I was knowing enough to be sure our worldly Uncle Geza must be at fault. Every one of his letters had started a crisis in our house.

I arrived to find the whole family in a solemn mood. My mother was red-eyed, as if she had been crying. When she saw me, she fought against it briefly but burst into tears again.

"Oh, my Joe!" she said. "My poor little boy!"

Everybody started to cry at once, except my father and me. I was completely puzzled. "Quiet, everyone!" my father ordered in his best patriarchal tone. His word was law and after a few more sniffles and sleeves across the face, order was restored.

"Close your mouth, son," he said to me in a kindly way, "and sit down." He waited till I sat. Then, almost as if he was addressing a meeting (which, come to think of it, he *was*) he said: "Children, we have just received another letter from your dear uncle and my dear brother-in-law, Geza. He is in a place called Philadelphia in America. I will read you part of his letter, my children.

" 'You have so many children. I have none. How can you keep them all at your side and permit me to have not a one? After all, am I not the brother of your dear wife, the flesh of her flesh?' " My father looked at us all and folded the letter. "There is more like that too. Your mother and I have decided Uncle Geza is right. The question is, Who shall it be? Who is going to join him in America?"

All the girls started to weep. In Hungary in those days any girl was a financial burden on the family until she could be married and she was always a likely candidate when it came to sending someone away. "Now, now," said my father. "Let there be no tears. I have read much about that country and it sounds like a wonderful place, but I understand that women go out and walk alone on the streets there. I couldn't send a daughter of mine to such an immoral place."

The girls sighed with relief. My father's eye fell on his sons. "Emil," he said.

"Papa," Emil said, like a plea that he should not be exiled.

"Emil, I can't send you. After all, you are my eldest. Uncle Geza could not expect me to do that, could he?"

I knew what was coming, so I had to begin to prepare my counterattack. "Why not?" I asked.

"Quiet," ordered my father again. He turned to the youngest boy, Johnny. "And I couldn't send my youngest son away. Think how it would hurt his mother. He is still a baby." Johnny wasn't a baby by a long shot and he always hated it when we teased him and called him a baby, but he didn't seem to mind it at all now. He turned to me and grinned from one ear to the other.

"I don't want to go!" I announced, springing to my

feet. "I don't want to be the one!" I stretched out my hands to my mother. "Please, mama!" She opened her arms for me and I ran to her.

My father came over to where my mother was embracing me. "It is selfish of me," he said, "but I couldn't even bear to lose one son."

We all started to cry, even my father. We were happy that the family was not going to be broken up. That's the only explanation I can offer for the tears.

And yet, as the months passed, I knew that sooner or later I would be sent away from home. Uncle Geza would keep on asking for one of us, with all the cleverness of a big-city character who always got what he wanted. Finally, I would be sent away.

This made me, despite what I told the others, just a little curious about the place called America. My principal source of information came from the old Nick Carter books. They had been translated into Magyar and I began to read them hungrily, at first because I told myself I was learning about America. Later, because I found myself liking the way Americans lived. They went around killing each other a good deal but if you were lucky enough to be on Nick's side, it seemed to be a much more interesting existence than Szilagy-Somlyo offered.

I revealed my mixed feelings about America to my teacher, a man named Schwarz. In our town each religious community had its own school system. The curriculum was set down by the government and we all studied the same subjects, but Jews, Catholics and Protestants attended their own schools.

Schwarz, who had privately told me that he didn't approve of this system, said that in America this wasn't so. That was why he wanted to go there, he said dreamily. "I'm too old," he mused. "But I would like to have had a Protestant teacher or to have taught a Catholic child. It would have been an interesting experience." Schwarz became quite flushed and eloquent when he talked to me about America. He liked me. He had learned to trust my bargaining ability and my discretion. Schwarz had a secret vice. He drank. I never blamed him. He had seventy pupils, of all ages. He was a poet, a dreamer, a philosopher, but this didn't impress the schnapps-dealers—not that I could have told them for whom I was buying anyway. On what he made as a teacher, he not only had to be discreet, he had to be careful. Still, I think he liked me. He could read five languages and he could spin such wonderful yarns that I often missed my supper just to listen to him talk. And when you missed supper at my house, you missed it for good.

Schwarz began to tell me about an America that was different from Nick Carter's. Schwarz talked about the West where there was still land a man could get for nothing. On lovely spring afternoons, when I returned from the market with his bottle, he would take me to the river bank and read from a volume called *Leaves of Grass*. He translated for me, every word, line by line. I could feel the spirit of Walt Whitman, the clear, democratic love for all God's creatures, and I began to feel a part of it, even in Central Europe.

Sometimes Schwarz grew too eloquent about it. "Go on, boy!" he'd say. "Go to America! Leave home if you must! Go West—clear the land! Start now!" He made it seem urgent. I noticed this usually happened when the bottle was almost empty. I learned that I could stall the moment of decision if I watered what I bought for him a little.

Years later I went to see Schwarz and confessed what I had done. "I knew all the time," he said, half-smiling. He was an old man then and he had seen his dreams melt away. "But I didn't mind too much. Like you, I was content to talk about my dreams and not to follow them."

He was never quite as passive as he made himself sound later. He was always telling me that I didn't belong in a small town. "You're naturally restless. You'll never be a tradesman or a merchant, a *shammas* or a rabbi." He took a swig from the slivovitz I'd brought him and when he found it was empty, he looked at it wistfully and shrugged. "Some people hear music and it does nothing to them. But you will hear the music one day, mark my words, and it will speak to you, it will tell you something very secret, very private. Listen to the music, boy, and if it tells you to go somewhere, go."

It was something like being told that one should be prepared to fly to another planet. I don't wonder I shivered when he talked, but I think Schwarz did too.

3. Showman

IT was a beautiful town. There was only one street and when it rained the mud was calf-deep, but none of the boys minded that. It was not a ghetto town. As I have said, the population was about evenly divided among the three great faiths, with perhaps a few more Protestants. The result of this was that the Jews and Catholics bore equally whatever "discrimination" existed.

In the summer we went swimming in the river; in the winter we made primitive ice skates out of pieces of wood and we went skating. There were orchards in the farms around the town and when the fruit was ripe on the branches, we knew how to get the best of it. It taught us to be keen and to fend for ourselves. Those peasants loved every last apple on the branches.

Then there were the gypsies. There are gypsies all over the world but there are none like the Hungarian gypsies. They lived in a little community just outside our village. They were dirty, but a boy would not hold that against them. Everybody in town said they were shiftless and lazy, and, far from denying it, the gypsies justified it. "Why

17

should I go to work today?" I heard one of them say once. "We've got enough food for supper."

"But what about tomorrow? You have nothing to eat tomorrow."

The gypsy waved his hand impatiently. "That's tomorrow. Today I'm all right."

The gypsy girls were beautiful. They painted their faces; they wore their hair loose about the shoulders. They did not bathe much but in their wanderings they had found cheap perfumes which they liked to use in overpowering quantities. When they did bathe, by the way, it was at the river's edge, in broad daylight, laughing and giggling and splashing each other. It was all wild and romantic but what we kids saw usually made us run for home, believe it or not.

It was a beautiful town but I became aware of the poverty by the time I was ten. My mother was always having children and there was one whom I never saw and one who died when I was very young. My father had to walk a mile and a half each way, twice a day, to open and close the synagogue, in winter and summer. My mother, whom I remember as a beautiful woman, began to grow weary with childbearing and raising a big family on what came to ten dollars a month, my father's salary.

Our house consisted of two rooms, and, with a stray relative or two, there were usually ten of us who called it home. We drew water from a well and kept chickens and ducks and if a visitor from the big city had passed it, he would surely have said, "How quaint and charming."

But before I was ten I had awakened in the night and heard my mother weeping about the lack of food in the house. During the day she never let on. She smiled and urged us to eat everything on our plates and to take more, as mothers always do. I realized she was playing a game with us.

My father's wish was that I should become a rabbi. But, though I loved him and felt honored by his opinion of me, it never appealed to me.

I asked Schwarz about this. "Why don't you want to be one?" he asked me.

"I don't know," I said. "They are so poor. The poor are like slaves."

"Those who haven't money are always slaves to it," the teacher said. "A rabbi doesn't need money."

"It isn't only the money," I said. "I like trying new things, doing new things. But the money is a part of it, even so."

I started my first business venture about that time. On Friday evenings—the Sabbath—it was customary for the members of our community to eat fish. It came from a village some twenty miles away and was handled by one man. It occurred to me, as I did my singing huckstering in the market, that every other businessman had at least one competitor. The fishmonger had none. He was a beady-eyed man, fat with prosperity and contemptuous of his customers. If they complained of his prices, he shouted at them and told them to go away. If a family had no money, they got no fish, no matter how long he had known them, or what their trouble.

I began by telling the merchants I worked for that they were not paying me enough. I had been getting one

19

kroner, or about twenty-five cents, and I soon got two. I started saving.

It was winter when I had my capital. I rented a horse and wagon and drove to the town where fish could be bought. I don't think I've ever been as cold in my life. The steam was coming out of the horse's lungs in big puffs and when I sat on the wagon, I froze, but when I tried to walk beside the horse, I could not keep up with him.

On Friday morning I was at the market, in business for myself. I set a fair price for my fish and by noon was sold out.

The next week I had enough capital to come back to town with a larger amount of fish. Word had got out that my prices were lower and the housewives woke up early to come to my stall before I was sold out. As a result, my business boomed. I had to promise those who came too late that on the following week I would buy in larger quantities.

During that week, however, Schwarz called my name out in school one day. He was wearing a very long face and I had the feeling that he no longer approved of me.

"What's this I hear you've been doing?"

I did not know what he was talking about.

"The poor old fishmonger went to the rabbi and complained," he said. "He says it's unfair what you've been doing. For twenty-five years he's had the monopoly and now you want to take it away from him."

"I don't want to take it away from him," I said, almost tearfully.

Suddenly Schwarz grinned. I hadn't known he was teasing me. "You should take it away from him if you can,

Joe. The sanctimonious old fraud's been overcharging the people in this town long enough. Of course you'll have to justify yourself to the rabbi." In the communities of those days the rabbi was our judge of law, ethics and morality, as well as our spiritual guide. I knew the rabbi could stop me if he chose.

We had a very formal trial. The fishmonger had an arbitrator for his side. In turn, I had one. My father came with me, rather proud, I felt, that I dared to stand up to an established businessman. The fish man began by saying that for twenty-five years he had been serving the Jewish community. It was a matter of pride, he said, that he had been chosen in this humble way to serve God. Now, as he was pursuing his calling an upstart youngster had upset the delicate balance between him and his Maker. "This not a business," he said. "This is a service I render to the people."

It was the kind of argument that sounded pretty impressive. The rabbi was a selfless man and I wouldn't blame him for not approving of a youngster who dared to stand up against an older man. But my father smiled at me when it came my turn to speak; he nodded by way of encouragement.

I began by saying that I hadn't meant to hurt the fishmonger. "But after all our town has grown since he started and there is room enough for two of us. I'm not doing this to hurt anybody. I'm only trying to help my family. I'm making money to help them."

The fishmonger got to his feet. "See what I mean?" he shouted. "I do it as a service. I'm losing money every week and yet I don't care as long as I can help my people."

21

The rabbi stroked his chin thoughtfully. "If you're losing money," he said, "why don't you give it up? This is a good opportunity for you."

"But I can't!" the fishmonger protested. "I've got to make a living somehow."

I might have stayed on in the fish business indefinitely, but something happened that changed all our lives. A man by the name of Prinzip assassinated the Archduke Franz Ferdinand, heir to the throne of the Austro-Hungarian Empire. The First World War started. The farmers stopped bringing their produce into town. It was impossible for me to find fish to sell.

One day, a man in an army uniform came into our village. The men were lined up and those who looked like good prospects for the army were there and then told to report. My father, tall and erect, was among the first selected.

It did not matter that his family consisted of six living children and a wife. No consideration was given to them, or how he would provide for them, or what they would do in his absence. He was mobilized, and that was it.

A few days before he was to leave, my father called me into the kitchen. He closed the door so we would be alone. "I am not thinking of myself," he said, "but I must ask you to make a terrible sacrifice, Joe."

My father had never asked me to do anything for him and I could not imagine that he would ask me to do anything that would hurt me in the slightest.

"A boy your age should be going to school or learning a trade," he went on. "If you haven't got a trade, if there isn't something you can do to earn a living, the future will never be bright. I'm asking you to give that up," he went on.

He had taken up the matter of supporting his family with the congregation. Their solution had been that if some member of his family could continue to perform the duties of the *shammas,* they would see to it that my father's pay would go to the family.

It was a full-time job, my father explained. He'd been planning to see to it that at least I could learn a trade. The war might go on for years. When, and if, he returned, I'd be too old to learn a craft.

"We'll worry about that then," I told him.

So I became a *shammas.* My father's pay came to something like ten dollars a month. I took my duties very solemnly. I kept the books. I opened the *schul* at dawn and closed it at dusk. I thought I was doing fine. But I wasn't.

I arrived home one Friday evening to find my mother in tears.

"What's the matter?" I asked her.

"I never thought it would happen," she replied. "Here it is Friday, the Sabbath eve, and we do not have a *barchas.*" *Barchas* was a white ritual loaf of bread which was placed before the place of the head of the family at the Sabbath supper. White flour had become very expensive; prices of everything had gone up. The money I brought in was hardly enough to feed the family, let alone provide this.

"Wait a minute," I said.

I was gone about an hour. When I came back, I unwrapped a bundle and placed a *barchas* before my father's place.

"How did you get it?" my mother asked me.

"I got it."

My mother regarded me steadily for a long moment. Then she came over and put her arms around me. "My son," she said, "you will never be lost."

What I had done, I never told her. I went to a member of our congregation who was reputed to be the richest member. I told him of our situation. He gave me the loaf from his own table. For those fiscal advisers and agents of mine who are constantly trying to tie my hands down when it comes to lending money to friends, this episode may serve as an eloquent instance of why I do what I do. I think I can skip drawing the moral.

Another thing my benefactor told me I did not forget. "Joe," he said, "I've heard you at the market. I've seen you in business. Why don't you try to be as smart a *shammas* as you are a businessman?"

I thought about that a good deal. One thing was sure, I didn't propose to let my mother down when it came to the ritual loaf on Friday night. Another thing was that with prices going up and the salary remaining fixed, it would not stretch to provide the *barchas.*

When I arranged the details of a marriage or a *briss,* it was customary to give the *shammas* a small tip. Maybe, I thought, I could do my job and get a somewhat bigger gratuity. But how? I decided that most of the people who attended these functions were so stupefied by the length and dullness of the affairs that a tip was only perfunctory.

Someone once asked me when I started being a showman. I thought of my singing commercials in the market-place, but anyone could have done that. My first real production was a marriage. I decided to make this the most beautiful marriage that had ever taken place in our village.

I began even before the ceremony. When I saw the bride's father, I sang her praises. "I have never seen a more beautiful bride." The bridegroom's father I told: "What a handsome son you have." On the day of the wedding I told their mothers how beautiful their own off-spring were and how fortunate they each were in this marriage. Word got around in the families that this was no mere routine marriage. The young *shammas,* who was an old hand at weddings, was being carried away by this event. It made everybody in the family feel good inside. This made the mood of the whole wedding beautiful.

So far, so good. Now I had to do a little work on the script. Our rabbi had a tendency to confuse quantity with quality. Since the occasion was serious, he also had the idea that it ought to be handled solemnly and at great length. I told him to hurry things up because the couple had to catch a train. He protested that it might be unfair to leave out anything.

"Just this once," I begged him.

The marriage ceremony was over in half the time. Instead of being deadened, the guests were still lifted by the mood I'd created. Both fathers and two grandfathers sought me out and pressed a little something in my hand. Everybody said it was a most beautiful wedding. Even the rabbi turned to me privately. "You know," he said, "I think it's better this way."

25

As a *shammas*-producer I wasn't so good where funerals were concerned, but then, as I've already confessed, my natural inclination isn't toward tragedy anyway. But when it came to *brisses,* if I do say so myself, I was a great showman. I had different people primed to make little comments. "My, what a beautiful boy!" I would say, in loud, clear tones right where the parents and grandparents (and, if possible all the great-grandparents) could hear. They would all beam and glow. A friend who was a member of my cast would look at them all and say something like, "What do you expect, isn't he just the image of his mother?" If the family was well-to-do, I might even have a third actor say the baby looked more like the father. This made *everybody* happy. It cost me a kroner or two more, but it was worth it because it always got me a bigger tip.

Oh, I was a smart one, all right. But I will say this: from the time I got started, my mother never had to weep again when she sat down to the Sabbath supper.

4. *Money and Love*

SOME years ago I was laid up in bed. A distinguished Hungarian playwright came over to help me pass the time. I knew him from Europe and, while I was grateful for his company, I had never had much faith in his talent or his ability. He told me that it was a pity that he and I had never made a picture together. He had his wit and his sharp perception of people and I had whatever I had. (I don't think he got too specific on that point.)

It was so nice having him around that I leaned back against the pillow and said that there was a story I'd always wanted to do. What did he think of it? I outlined a basic situation and wove a couple of interesting (I thought) characters in and out of it.

The playwright didn't think much of my idea.

Four weeks later the same story was submitted to me. The playwright's name was on the cover. I still thought it a pretty good story, even though he had changed his mind, and I didn't want to say anything about our having talked about it before. I got in touch with Charlie Feldman, the author's agent, a man of unqualified and passionate enthusiasms, and I told Charlie I thought the story was pretty interesting and I'd buy it for five thousand dollars.

Charlie called me back. "Joe," he said, "it's far too good a story to sell for so little. I'm prepared to give ten thousand for it myself."

"I'm sorry," I replied. "Five's about all it's worth to me."

Sure enough, Charlie bought the story for ten thousand. I called my friend-playwright. "You can't do this to me," I said. "You know it's my story and I told it to you and I'm even giving you five thousand for my own story."

"I know, Joe," he said. "I know. But why should I sell it for five if I can get ten? You wouldn't want me to lose money on the deal, would you?"

I had to admit he had me there.

It isn't easy turning a dollar in this world and there are far too many disputes, lawsuits, and recriminations. I take this tolerant view not so much that I wish to dispute learned professors of ethics but because I had a brief and, come to think of it, fairly successful fling in the world of business myself. I soon learned that all sorts of things were permissible which my father would never have condoned.

It happened this way. Staging my little productions as *shammas* brought in a little money but not enough to keep pace with the rising cost of living. The peasants were not bringing their produce into the village because they knew, as the war went on, inflation would get worse and worse. Money might be valueless but a bushel of wheat or beans was something that would always be worth something.

28

The army met this lack of cooperation among the peasants of rounding up youngsters in the villages, giving them some money, and sending them out individually to the farms to buy a bushel or two of whatever the peasants had. For this, each boy was rewarded with a kroner. It seemed like an easy way to make some extra money, so I went out with the boys.

The man in charge of this was a sergeant and it was his custom to come to our village once a week. He was a lazy man and he'd no sooner get us boys off than he would head for a café. The thing he liked about his job was that it got him away from headquarters for the day. He didn't like all the detail connected with it, however. The cashier at the café was the prettiest girl—I should say, the *next* prettiest—girl in town and the sergeant hated to leave her side.

One day I took my father's salary and some of the tip money I'd saved, and rounded up the boys. I spread my capital around and told the boys to go out and do their buying. When the sergeant came that week, he found his work had been done for him, and while it cost a little more than he'd expected, he didn't care. It wasn't his money.

The next week it cost even more. Law of supply and demand, I explained. Besides, wasn't all the trouble of rounding up boys and keeping records and such off his hands? Wasn't that worth something?

It certainly was. I was in business with the army.

As the war dragged on, there were fewer marriages, what with most of the young men being drafted into the army and never coming home on leave. Fewer marriages, fewer births. I got so involved with business that I engaged two of my best friends to take care of the actual physical work of being a *shammas*. They opened the place in the morning, swept the floor, gathered the prayer books. Their names were Mortzie and Lojosh, two huge boys with hands as hard as horseshoes and bodies to match. They were almost feeble-minded but they were so sweet and kind that I loved them as I loved my brothers.

I was in business. Buying for the army, I noticed there were all sorts of things in short supply. People felt you were doing them a favor if you could bring back something that the war had made it hard to find.

One month I made as much as five hundred dollars. No, this is not a typographical error. It was a great deal of money in Hungary then. I lost some of it the next month when I bought a carload of potatoes and found when they were unloaded that every last one of them was rotten. I lost some more of it when some deals I played along with didn't pan out. But, as I say, I learned a few things too, notably that in business in wartime anything goes. In a nice way, I mean, of course.

For example, one time I learned there was a shortage of a local product called *rezor*. *Rezor* was a depilatory in great use by the orthodox Jews in our town who were forbidden, by some Talmudic rule, ever to shave. The men could use this chemical but were not allowed to touch blade to face. As the war went on, *rezor* became almost unavailable. Beards in town grew longer. It seemed to me that if one could find *rezor*, he might be able to turn a nice profit.

I went to the storekeeper who used to handle the stuff. "Would you be interested," I asked him, "if I could get you any *rezor*?"

"But of course. I don't think you can get any. I've tried and tried. If you can, I'll take it, definitely."

Shortly after that my business took me to Budapest. I was lucky enough to find almost two hundred pounds of *rezor*. I bought the whole lot and could hardly wait to get back to my storekeeper friend.

"I've got it," I announced eagerly. "I've got enough for years!"

"*Ach*—too bad. The men in this town have gotten used to their beards now. I can't use it any more."

"But, please—you don't understand. I've got a lot of money tied up in it. I'll let you have it for what I paid for the stuff."

He wasn't interested in it at any price. Today, when I've had some experience with this kind of bargaining (it's a little bit like buying a literary property for a film, in which you, as a producer, have expressed some interest) I'd understand the position he was trying to put me in for bargaining purposes. What he was trying to do, of course, was to cut me right down to profitable size. Profitable for him, that is.

I suffered for several hours. It even pained me that I hadn't sprouted the beginnings of a beard myself, so *I* could use the *rezor*. Then I had an idea. I saw a stranger in town and gave him a kroner to go into the store and ask for *rezor*. He was to say he was a big buyer from another town who'd be willing to take all of the stuff the storekeeper could get for him.

So, bright and early the next morning the storekeeper arrived at our house. "You little rascal, you've caused me a lot of trouble," he said, smiling broadly at me. "I told my wife about what you did and she says it isn't fair to you. I'll take that stuff off your hands. I want peace in the family. What'd you pay for it?"

Among other lessons I learned that day was this: one of life's choicer satisfactions is to outsharp the sharpie. I played coy, insisted that I didn't want to burden him with a product that no one wanted and, besides, I even believed I might be able to dispose of the *rezor* myself. But he wanted it now, even to the extent of paying me twice what it had cost me in Budapest. So I sold it, finally.

I wondered what he thought when the big buyer from the neighboring town never showed up. Not that I lost any sleep about it, mind. Pulling *such* a stunt on a boy.

I was riding high. My suits were tailored in Budapest. I became the best-known character in our town. I moved my mother and my family to a somewhat bigger house. Often, when I returned from the big city, I would bring a bottle of good slivovitz to my old teacher. A true man of the world, Schwarz never approved or disapproved of what I was doing. "The only thing that matters, boy, is this: have you heard the music yet?"

Yes, I told him, I'd heard the great gypsies, the ones who play the fiddles and the cymbaloms in Budapest, and it was wonderful.

"What did they say to you?"

"I don't know," I told him honestly. "They just made me restless."

"And what else did you find in the big cities?"

I did not dare to admit that the big city frightened me. It was all right when I was dealing with merchants, but elsewhere I always had the feeling that I didn't belong, that a waiter might come up to me and ask me what the devil I was doing sitting at a table with the guests.

There was another thing I'd seen in Budapest, I told my former teacher, that stirred me. I'd been to a theater. It was like a music hall and what I liked best about it was the air of good humor, light talk, and fun. And the actors seemed to be enjoying themselves, too. Even when I'd made a bad business deal, I could go to this place and forget everything. There was an actor there who could make me laugh by saying something as simple as "What time is it?" His name was Sakall, Szoke Sakall, and he was tall and good-looking and he had something I could not describe.

"The word," Schwarz said, "is charm. Yes, you have been hearing the music." Then he paused. "But why have you come back?"

I avoided answering the question. I did not know how to tell him that I had fallen in love.

Her name was Rosika. I could not tell him about it because it was a beautiful and hopeless love. Despite my success in the world of business, despite my travels, despite the music I had heard in Budapest, where had I found true love? Right in my own home town.

She was the daughter of the police chief. I had seen the great beauties of Budapest, the painted and gorgeously dressed hussies of a wartime capital. Beside Rosika, these were as artificial as Meissen figurines.

33

Her father did not approve of me and I could be quite sure mine would not have approved of her, as she was not of my faith. That did not matter to me, or to her, but it meant a good deal to her father. He forbade us ever to see each other.

This had the effect of making our meetings even more romantic. We would meet at dusk and hold hands on the river bank. I would describe the glories of life in Budapest. I would tell her that nothing a man could see there was half so beautiful as she. No wonder she found me an agreeable companion.

Even when my business collapsed, she believed in me. As the might of the Central Powers was dragged in the dust, ruin overtook all of us. The little operators, like the sixteen-year-old boy from Szilagy-Somlyo, were wiped out. The inflation became so insane that nothing had any value, particularly money.

When peace came, we did not know for many weeks whether our father was dead or alive. Our town had been firmly placed inside Romania by the Treaty of Versailles. Then a letter came from my father and he told us that he was well and would be home soon. I had had a brilliant career in business and was now broke. We had another, somewhat bigger house, but I soon realized that this only had the effect of increasing our overhead.

And I was seventeen years old. Too old to go to school. Too late in my life to be an apprentice. I was in love with a girl whose father would as soon shoot me as look at me. Curiously enough my brothers and sisters still insisted on regarding me as a successful man. My best friends were

34

two sweet feeble-minded boys and a schoolteacher who talked wistfully of the fine brandies I used to bring him from the big cities. I was a failure and there was no future for me and I alone knew it. That was the worst of it.

5. *The Superannuated Shammas*

So now I began to think of going to America. It was the only way out for me. My father had returned from his service with the army. The war had, if anything, made him a more gentle, compassionate, and forgiving man. He did not talk about what he had done and what he had seen. It was his habit to take the most kindly and understanding view of people. His army service must have tested this to the utmost.

Naturally he resumed his duties as *shammas*. The boundary confusions brought on by the Versailles Treaty, the mutual hatred and recriminations involved in a defeated cause—everything made trade impossible.

Somewhere, in his army service, my father had picked up a copy of Lincoln's Gettysburg Address. It seems strange but he kept it with his prayer things. It was in a German translation but even in that language my father said the words had a biblical quality. He read it to me and I remembered old Schwarz reading Walt Whitman. It was then I decided I had to go to America.

My father said: "My son, the worst thing about the war

was being away from all my family. I do not think I could bear it if you left me."

Rosika said life would not be worth living if I were to leave.

Only Schwarz told me to go. He did so not directly but by asking me why I thought I wanted to live in America. He was really a fine teacher. In any event, I remember telling him of my dream of America.

"Here, when people are sick or in trouble, no one helps," I said. "If you get very sick, you die. But over there, I don't know why, I get the feeling people *care*. If you are in trouble, they help. Everybody belongs to the country, and the country belongs to everybody. It's like a big family. I don't know why or how. I just sense it. I don't believe that in America anybody has to walk in the mud. I have a feeling that something is different there."

"Very well, when are you leaving? What is holding you back?"

I told him about my father. He understood that. Unorthodox as he was, Schwarz knew that in our world a father's wish was always paramount.

"You must make him want you to leave."

This happened a few months later, in a way we never anticipated. It was my father's custom, as with the other men in our town, to gather in a coffee house at the end of the day to read the papers, to discuss the day's events, and to pass the time among friends. As *shammas*, my father was also able to settle his accounts then with members of his congregation.

It was late fall. I usually came to the coffee house to accompany my father home. He asked me to wait while

37

he finished a discussion with friends. The sun had set hours before. The rains had been heavy that year and we had to walk carefully in the slippery mud.

"What have you been doing all day?"

I shrugged my shoulders. I had wasted the day, visiting friends, chatting with the gypsies outside of town. All my days were like that then. It wasn't the kind of thing my father would have liked to hear.

From out of the dark we could see an enormous figure. He staggered toward us, lurching and slipping in the mud and mumbling as he came in a way that told us he was drunk. As he approached, we could tell he was a peasant. "Now, now, you just wait a minute!" he called to us.

When he reached us, he swayed before my father and then reached out and seized my father's beard in his fist. "Well, well, a man who doesn't shave. Must be a Jew?" he taunted my father.

As I have said, there was little anti-Semitism in our town. The old men had told tales of such things, but it was always in another place and in another time. There was friction, of course, between the groups, but it was minor. The shock of what was taking place and the indignity to which my father was being subjected almost froze me.

"You must take your hands off me, friend," my father said to the peasant, very gently. There was no anger in his voice.

"Am I hurting you?" the peasant replied, pulling the beard hard. I could see the pain on my father's face but he said nothing.

"Let my father go," I said.

"Oh, he's your father? And don't you like to see me pull his beard?" He tugged again, harder than ever.

I scarcely reached the peasant's shoulders but I swung out and slapped his face as hard as I could. It was like striking at a wall but it had the effect of surprising the stranger and making him let go of my father. He lurched angrily and unsteadily after me.

I was small enough to duck and elude him. I came up to my father. "Go on home, father," I told him.

"This is wrong," my father said. He was opposed to violence for any reason. In his view it was never justified. It was not the way I felt. The drunk stumbled into us. I was able to trip him slightly, so he lost his balance, and so did my father, who fell down. The drunk swerved and came back toward me. I left my father's side. The drunk looked at my father but he had become more interested in the little fellow who had dared to slap him. I did not want to run because then I knew he would go after my father again.

I stood my ground. He came at me, grabbing my coat and pulling me toward him as if I were a rag doll. He brought my face close to his and then pushed me into the mud. I fell hard. I could see him come toward me again. I tried to reach my feet in the slippery mire but I kept falling down. Then my hand fell on something hard. I seized it. A big rock. I backed away and got to my feet.

"Look out," I said when he came at me. He swung. I ducked and when he was off balance I hit him with the rock. When he went down it was like a sack of grain falling from a wagon. I thought I had killed him.

39

"You shouldn't have done that," my father said, bending down over the man. For my part, I would have done it again. My father would have found an excuse for anybody or anything.

"Come on, father." I put my hands under his arms and lifted him to his feet. I didn't want him around.

When we got home, my mother could tell we had been in a fight. He told her what had happened. "Joe must go away," she said.

"Where to?" my father asked.

"To America," my mother said firmly. Then to me: "Do you want to go there?"

"Yes, I think I do."

My father shook his head. "He must go away. But not so far. I do not want him to go an ocean away. I have a friend who is a diamond cutter in Antwerp. He can go there."

We learned, the next day, that I had not killed the drunken peasant. I had no regrets, however. If killing him had been the price of saving my father the humiliation he suffered at the hands of this lout, I think I would have done just what I did. That he had not died did not change our plans. My parents might have been afraid that when he recovered, he might come after me again. I knew him for a drunken bully and I wasn't afraid of him, with or without a rock in my hand. But I was ready to leave this town. Life gave me no alternative.

My father sold his gold watch and the small watch and gold chain that hung at my mother's neck and which she had inherited from her own mother.

Schwarz was glad. "I'll miss you, boy," he said. I don't

think any student ever got a better compliment from his teacher.

Rosika and I played it à la Romeo and Juliet—though I didn't know it, of course, at the time.

"Promise you won't forget me?"

"I promise. I will make a huge success and send for you."

"You're just saying it."

"No. You are the most wonderful, the most beautiful." Et cetera. Et cetera.

It sounds foolish now but we both played our parts fully. All I know is that I meant it with every bit of sincerity of which I was capable. This was it, this was for real, this was for keeps. I wasn't going to be able to write because her father might find out and then there'd be the devil to pay, but she need have no fear that I'd forget her.

During my last days at home, when I knew I was leaving, everything in our town took on an appearance of the most unbelievable loveliness. I walked along the river where in winter I had skated on wooden ice skates and where in summer I had lain on my back while Schwarz read to me and drank from his schnapps bottle. The village took on a storybook quality, the little streets and houses and the mountains that surrounded it, beginning, at this season, to be topped with snow. I was sure that I would never see anything as beautiful.

The day my train was to leave, my father said nothing to me. He kept looking at me. I could not desert him, I thought. I would go to Antwerp, after all, as he wanted me to. He gave me Uncle Geza's address and told me he had written his brother-in-law that I was leaving home and was going to learn the trade of cutting diamonds. But that was all he said to me that last day.

My train was to leave at three in the morning. At twelve he put on his coat, told me to get ready.

"You've got three hours," my mother said.

"The train might be early," my father said. "Let's go, Joe."

I said goodbye to my mother and my brothers and sisters. I walked to the station beside my father. He insisted on carrying my bags. We said nothing.

The station was dark, deserted. We walked up and down the platform, still not talking. Later, much later, when the station master arrived to make his preparations, and we could see the light flicker on in his office, my father knew the moment of our parting was not far away.

"If I would have been a better man, a more aggressive man, you would not have to be doing this," he said. I tried to stop him, but he shook his head, smiling gently.

"I do not mind saying these things," he said simply, refusing to be stopped. "I guess I did fail you and all my children. I have never sought money because I have preferred to serve God, but what did I do for my own children? I have not been able to give you an education, and you could not even learn a trade because you had to take my place."

"That is not so, father. You have taught me many things and have given me more."

He put his arms around me. "I will not tell you what to do in life," he said. "But never forget God."

The train was pulling in. It was a branch line and I would have to make a change in a few hours. The train

42

was a tiny thing, chugging and puffing like a toy. From the locomotive's stack there came a shower of sparks—it was a wood-burning affair. When it came to a stop, it did so with a clanging of metal.

"Go, my son," my father said. "Remember that not a single day of my life will pass without thinking of you and praying for you."

I held back the tears for his sake. I went into the third-class carriage. I could see him on the platform, his wonderful face, with his clear blue eyes and his reddish beard, a beautiful face full of a lifetime of kindness and loving, like the Renaissance portraits of Jesus. He was waving to me when the train pulled out. I think he must have known I had no intention of going to Antwerp.

6. Champagne and Cops

It was to be America after all. Maybe I knew it all the time; maybe I was fooling myself because I could never lie to my father. He told me once, "You never have to remember the truth." What he meant was that when you lie you always have to remember the story you made up. Tell the truth and you don't have to cover your tracks.

Hamburg was the port I made for. I had a transit visa. Hundreds of us were herded into barracks until passage could be arranged. There wasn't much money left from the gold watches my father and mother sold; certainly not enough for steamship fare. But Uncle Geza was in America. His address was 211 W. 8 Street, Philadelphia. I cabled him, sat back and waited for my ticket to arrive.

Many of us were in that fix. The German government which was having its own problems only a year or so after the end of the first war, didn't want us, penniless, and supposedly in transit only. We haunted the post office and the cable office, and as our permitted length of stay drew to an end and our tickets did not arrive, we began avoiding anybody who might cast a fishy eye on us and ask to see our papers.

I had a friend of about my age who was also waiting for a ticket from America. His name was Jack Biegeleisen and he was going to New York. His cable was addressed to 411 W. 111 Street. He got no reply either.

We were in the barracks one day when we learned that the authorities had decided to send all those who had no money, no steamship tickets and whose transit papers had expired back to their point of origin. That was all Jack and I had to hear. Taking only a few things, we let ourselves out by a back window, ran across a roof, and dropped to a deserted side street.

My suitcases dated back to my more prosperous days and I had some clothes in them. I sold them all and we were able to eat for a few days. We had to move warily. When you are looking for a policeman, of course, you never see a one; if you want to see them at every corner, in every alley and doorway, coming out of the remotest bushes and shrubbery of the city parks, just go on the lam. Everywhere we turned there were police.

The more you avoid them, the more suspect you seem to look. A glaze comes into your eyes that tells policemen you don't want to have anything to do with them and, of course, that's an invitation to ask what you're doing. In our case, they also wanted to see our papers. Luckily for us, the Hamburg police force was beefier and a lot older than we. Fences stopped them and dark doorways fooled them.

Every day, when the coast was clear, we went to the cable office. No, no reply. I could not understand why my Uncle Geza had not wired me. Nor could Jack figure out why his ticket had not come.

45

"Are you sure you sent the cable?" we asked the clerk. He told us to get out before he called the police.

We slept in doorways, on park benches, and in abandoned sheds. It was getting cold; still, sleep wasn't the big problem. We weren't eating. Then one day we met Siggy.

Siggy was obviously a young man of means. He dressed like a fashion plate; he talked to clerks and such in an airy fashion. We met him on one of our daily visits to the cable office and when he heard of our plight, he congratulated us. Weren't we having the time of our life in Hamburg? he asked. Wasn't it a great town to be stuck in? The clerk was counting out a tremendous number of bills that had been telegraphed to Siggy.

We told him we didn't like Hamburg at all, that the cops were looking for us, that we hadn't bathed in weeks, and unless we got something to eat soon, we'd be glad to be sent back home.

"You poor chaps," Siggy said. He talked like that. "Come, be my guests for the evening."

We went to his hotel room and cleaned up a little. He told us he too was on his way to America, but he was having such a fine time in Hamburg that he was simply staying on. When he ran out of money, he'd wire home and say he needed more if he was to get to America. They kept sending him remittances every time he wired. "I guess they're anxious to be rid of me," he said, chuckling at his good fortune.

We went out to dinner in the best restaurant in town. But first we must have champagne, Siggy insisted. There was quite a to-do about the brand and the year. We didn't care. The room smelled deliciously of roasts and rich

46

gravies. "Drink up, boys," Siggy said. "There's a lot more where this comes from."

By the fifth bottle we began to understand Siggy's airy manner. It became clear that the only nourishment he had taken since he left home had been champagne. When Jack and I hinted that something with a little more bulk to it would go well along about here, Siggy got annoyed.

"Peasants," he berated us. "Is that all you can think of? Stuffing your stomachs? Come, have another bottle."

We had two more bottles. The price of each would have fed Jack and me for a week. We began to protest that our hunger was unbearable.

Siggy grew angry. He got to his feet, steadying himself as though the floor beneath him was rocking. "You fellows disappoint me," he said thickly. "I thought you were my friends, but you have failed me. You are fair-weather friends, that's all. All you want is wretched, greasy food."

He was so upset that he called for the check, settled and staggered out.

Jack and I walked out minutes later. Siggy was waiting for us. He threw his arms about us both and wept copiously. "I'm sorry, friends," he said. "I shouldn't have lost my temper. Come, be my guests. Let us have some more champagne."

"We're too hungry to drink any more," said Jack.

"Oh, my God," said Siggy in despair. And he weaved down the street to another café.

The next day we were desperate. We found there were jobs out in the country as potato-diggers. "Meals provided," we were told.

47

"The way I feel I would pick coal with my bare hands for a meal," I said. "Let's go."

Before they fed us, they put us to work. Blame it on our hunger, sleeping in cold, hard doorways; maybe we had been weakened by our session with Siggy. In any case, Jack and I almost dropped in the fields. The only thing that kept us on was the thought of "meals provided."

When the day was over, they gave us the meal, as promised. I don't know why we were surprised that it turned out to be potato soup.

"I think it was better starving," Jack said, sampling the stuff.

He was right, but we ate enough anyway for a dozen men. Then we went back to town. At the telegraph office there was still no word for me. I sent a wire to Uncle Geza's brother in Budapest: WHAT IS UNCLE GEZA'S ADDRESS IN AMERICA? I got a prompt reply: 211 W. 8 Street, Philadelphia. The clerk brought out his copy of my original wire. It read 2 II W. 8 Street. "There couldn't be two hundred and eleven houses on one street," he explained, "not even in America." He had done the same service for Jack.

"Please," we begged him, "just send it our way." "Very well," he said, "if you want to waste your money." We gave him every pfennig we had earned in the potato fields.

When we came out of the telegraph office, we heard a voice shout, "Hey!" We didn't even turn to look. Reacting like the hunted men we were, we ran. The voice ran right after us. But when it called us, "Friends! Dear friends!" we turned to look.

It was Siggy. He came up to us, holding on to our

shoulders to catch his breath. "I don't blame you for wanting to avoid me," he said. "Am I glad to see you! Where have you been?"

When we told him, he clucked sympathetically. "You poor fellows. Come, let's go into that café."

We went in and once more he started ordering champagne. This time I decided not to suffer. I drew the waiter aside. "What's he paying for the wine?" It came to about five dollars a bottle. "How much'll you give me for a bottle?" He offered about a dollar. "It's a deal," I said.

Siggy was pleased with us. We didn't talk about food and we ordered wine hand over bucket. "This is the best evening I've ever had since I left home. I must wire for more money tomorrow."

When we said good night to him, we had enough for a little something to eat. I had a brief pang about the ethics of it. Then I realized why I was doing it. "I'm going to go to America," I told Jack. "Nothing is going to stop me. If I have to swim there, I'll swim. But I'm going there."

Three days—and I cannot even begin to estimate how many bottles of champagne—later, a wire arrived from my uncle. He had bought passage for me on the *Mount Clay,* of the Hamburg-American Line. Jack got his wire and ticket too.

"I still can't understand how they can have so many houses on one street," the telegraph office clerk insisted.

Siggy saw us off. He brought several buckets of champagne to the dock and we had a real farewell party. I think we are possibly the only steerage immigrants who ever departed for America amid the popping of corks and the pouring of golden, vintage wine into crystal glasses.

49

7. The Making of an American

I ARRIVED in Philadelphia on a Tuesday. On Wednesday my Uncle Geza took me to the courthouse, where I applied for my first citizenship papers. On Thursday I went to work in a belt factory. My uncle lived among a number of Hungarian families, and they all spoke broken English. On Friday I announced that if they wished to speak to me they would have to speak English. I had no wish to speak Hungarian any more. I kept this vow so determinedly that when I returned to my native country eight years later, my Hungarian was so rusty that I had to take a refresher course before I could speak it again.

My first impression of America was disappointing. There were people here. They were poor. They arose in the early winter morning, went to work, came home when it was dark, lived in small rooms. Was this America? Where was the frontier Schwarz had told me about? Where were the big buildings, the big stores? Even the girls disappointed me. In 1921 they were painting their mouths in tiny cupid's bows, rouging their cheeks and arranging their hair with little curls around their ears and over their foreheads. They looked grotesque to a stranger.

But when I got my first paycheck, I began to understand the new country. In one week I was accepted as a member of the working force. I found $12.85 in my pay envelope. I sent two of it home, gave Uncle Geza five against what he laid out for my ticket, paid three dollars for my room (they didn't want it but I thought it better to get everything on a business basis) and I still had some money left. The next week I raised my production and my pay.

In a month I was asking my cousin, the foreman, how much he earned. "I pull down thirty-six a week," he told me proudly.

"How long have you been here?" I asked him.

"I've been working for the firm for sixteen years."

I made up my mind to look for another job. I was up to twenty a week and I didn't propose to wait sixteen years to get to thirty-six. My Americanization had begun.

There was a girl in the house next door whom I found very attractive. I bought an American suit and new shoes and an American shirt. I saved a few dollars and arranged to meet her.

"You speak English pretty well for a foreigner," she said.

"I'm not a foreigner," I explained. "I'm an American. I've got my first papers."

"You're still a foreigner."

"I'm more an American. I understand that in this country if you want to go out with a girl, you just ask her. Is that right?"

"See?" she teased. "You still think like a foreigner."

"I will learn. Give me a little time."

"Where will you take me if I go out with you?"

"You will have the best time you've ever had, I promise you."

"All right. I'll go out with you."

I worked harder than ever that week so I'd find more in my pay envelope. I buttonholed everybody about places to eat and dance. Not that I danced, but I didn't think that was necessary. On Saturday night I took her out. I arrived with a corsage. I had a taxi waiting outside. I did not discuss with her where we should go, or what we should do. I wanted to give the impression of a man who'd grown up in this world and who didn't need advice. The evening passed very well, I thought. At the end of it, she said: "You're not bad for a greenhorn."

I knew then I had to leave Philadelphia. There I would always be the stranger, the foreigner, the greenhorn. In Philadelphia I would live with other Hungarians and be part of their world. I wanted to make my own world.

I mentioned it to Uncle Geza. "Don't be ridiculous," he said. "You're still new in this country. Wait till you know your way around a little more."

"If I wait, I'll never go. I've seen it happen."

He still didn't think I should. But I left anyway, without his knowledge.

In New York I found it wasn't so easy to get a job. This surprised me a little. After all, hadn't I got a job in a belt factory on my second day? I'd forgotten that relatives had arranged for me to get the work. I found a room in back of a butcher shop on Eighty-second Street in Yorkville. My Philadelphia savings were running out fast when an advertisement in the paper drew my eye. They wanted toothpaste salesmen. This is for me, I thought. Everybody uses toothpaste; what could be easier?

The deal was very simple. All we had to do was persuade the druggists to stock our product. We salesmen got to keep the total proceeds of the first order. I took my sample case and started making the rounds. "I've got Colgate, Ipana, Squibb," the druggists told me. "I've got Dr. Lyon's, Pebeco, Forhan's, Pepsodent and Kolynos and Iodent, Number One and Two. I've got powders and stuff for dentures, so why would I want yours?"

"Because someone might come in and ask for it and if you didn't have it, you'd lose a sale."

"Young man, I'd switch them over to something I've got."

It went like that for two days. Then I remembered *rezor*. I rounded up several boys and offered them a few cents each. They were dispatched to the drug stores and told to ask for my product. If the druggist didn't have it, they were to go out. If the druggist tried to sell them something else, they were to say their mothers wouldn't have anything but my product in the house.

It worked pretty well too, but I could see there was no future in selling toothpaste. The next job was harder to find. Every time I answered an advertisement I found long lines of job-hunters ahead of me. I saw a classified ad that seemed to fill the bill perfectly. It was in the "Help Wanted, Male" section.

YOUNG MAN—Preferably recent arrival in this country. Must be able to cry profusely at will. Splendid opportunity to serve mankind and to advance himself. No overweight boys need apply.

53

I soon found out the reason for the last sentence. My employers told me I was made to measure for the job. They were a charitable organization, they told me, who toured the factories of New York, mostly during the lunch hour. They conducted meetings of the workers and raised money in behalf of starving peoples left in war-torn Europe.

I was to be a graphic instance of why the workers had to contribute. At a signal, I had to break into tears.

They hired four of us, but I was soon far and away the best of the lot. All spielers always asked for me. I cried magnificently. The speaker would point to me and relate a story about the starving Armenians or Greeks, about the terrible tragedy my tender eyes had seen, and I would weep. I got five dollars a day, better pay than I'd ever earned. While I knew the spielers were laying it on a little thick, I could not deny there was a certain poetic truth in what they said, despite the license they were taking. Having seen a little of what they said was happening, I could weep bucketsful, even though I was no Armenian or Greek, as they often said I was.

One Saturday I came to work to pick up my week's earnings but I found that a police wagon and a number of men sporting badges and carrying clubs were there before me. I was somewhat taken aback to see my erstwhile employers being bundled into the paddy wagon. Just somewhat. Evidently the proceeds of my crying fests had never gotten to the Armenians and the Greeks.

I was unemployed again. I was wearing out shoe leather on Sixth Avenue when I saw a long line of men waiting to be interviewed. It seems there were four dishwashers' jobs at a hotel in the Catskills and the jobs would be filled from these men.

"What hotel is it?"

They told me where it was. I took the next train up.

"I'm a dishwasher," I told them up there.

"Good. We've been waiting for you. There's a pile of dishes there. When are the others coming up?"

"Pretty soon, I guess."

When the other four came up, no one knew what to do. "I don't know about you fellows," the boss said, "but I know this guy's a good dishwasher." So they kept me on. During the rush I doubled as a busboy. In the evenings, after work, I could stand in the cool dark and hear the band play for the guests. The fireflies danced before my eyes. I thought of Schwarz. "Have you heard the music?" It was a different music, warm, gay; some of it reminded me of the gypsies at home, of people I had known, sadness I had felt. But there were new themes in it, too, and they stirred me greatly, for this was like no music I had ever heard before and it had simplicity and directness and honesty.

When the summer was over, I got a job as a busboy in a cafeteria just off Broadway and Forty-sixth Street. It was owned by one of the guests in the hotel. This job marks the turning point in my life. Right around the corner was a movie house. The ushers were our steady customers. We got to know each other. I'd get them extra helpings. They, in turn, told me to come and see them whenever I wanted to get in to see the movie.

I had a full working day. It started at seven in the morning, until nine-thirty. Then I had two hours off, started again at eleven-thirty and worked until two-thirty, when I had the afternoon off, until five-thirty. Then I worked until nine. The pay was good, though: sixteen dollars, and meals. And the movies were free.

The first picture I saw was *The Girl I Love* with Charles Ray. I had seen pictures before, not often, but enough so that they were not entirely new to me. Years before, in my home town, there had been a kind of road-show of a Danish picture, a "talking" picture, believe it or not. Two people hid behind the screen and uttered lines that the people on the film were supposed to be saying.

But I had never seen anything like *The Girl I Love*. Or anybody like Charlie Ray. I went back to see the picture no less than twenty-six times. I saw in this picture a home-spun quality that was intensely real to me. Charlie Ray was any boy: clumsy, willing, charming, inept, sad, funny.

I was suffering from a malady. I didn't know at that time of my life what it was, but I was movie-struck. I daydreamed and mooned and bought all the fan magazines and studied my face in the mirror this way and that to see if there was any resemblance between me and my heroes. I glowered at myself like Francis X. Bushman and tried to put on a shy and charming look like Richard Barthelmess. But my favorite was Charlie Ray. I read everything I could find about him. I modeled my life and my attitudes on what the fan-magazine writers said were his.

In fact, I admired him so much that I decided to follow him and go into the movies myself.

8. The Back Door

LARRY SEMON showed me how. I saw this young comedian, with the sad, hangdog look, on the screen and I told myself that if he could be an actor, so could I. He played a pathetic young man who was always making things worse when he thought he could help them. I looked in the mirror and told myself that if Larry Semon could make it, so could I.

There was another advertisement in the papers:

> MOVIE STARS—A guaranteed course of training for serious young people interested in making a career in this new field. Those interested apply at once.

When I presented myself, I was critically surveyed.

"He's not very tall," one of the school officials said.

"But he has blue eyes," another commented.

"Ah, yes, blue eyes. They're something of an advantage."

"Has a slight foreign accent."

"So has Valentino," another said. "But he's not the leading man type."

57

For a while I thought they were not going to accept me. I was ready to beg them to give me a chance.

"This is very serious work," one of the school officials told me. "We don't want to waste our invaluable training on irresponsible people."

"You won't," I assured them.

"Sober, reliable people, who've shown some evidence of their reliability. For example, people who own property, or have a savings account."

"I have a savings account."

"That's a very good sign. But a dollar or two in the bank doesn't necessarily show a sound character."

"I've got two hundred dollars saved." I had three hundred, but I was not a complete fool.

"Hm," said the official. "You realize the entrance fee is one hundred and fifty?"

"Yes, of course."

"And there'll be a weekly charge?"

"I don't mind. I've got a good job."

He stood up and took my hand. "Congratulations. In a few weeks you will be a full-fledged movie star."

The school was located in a third-floor loft of an old factory building in the West Thirties. The original charge was to be ten dollars a week, but when they saw I had exceptional talent—and a steady job—my instructors believed that I should gain what they called actual camera experience. The school did not own a real camera, but they had a tripod and someone fixed a kind of box on it. This raised my tuition to twelve dollars a week but we all agreed that it was worth every penny of it.

58

It wasn't the school so much as the other students who instilled confidence and assurance into me. I observed them and was forced to admit to myself that I outshone them all. If *this* was to be my competition, I was unquestionably destined for big, important things.

My heart was set on comedy. But I had more ability than I realized. My teachers wanted me to be a leading man too. They thought so much of my natural gifts that they were willing to give me what they called a working scholarship. One hundred dollars and a mere seven dollars a week for ten additional weeks.

I was flattered, but I stood firm. I was anxious to start my career at once. In the last weeks of the course, I quit my job as a busboy in the cafeteria. If I was to begin a new career, I did not want to hold back in any way.

My diploma looked like this:

INTERNATIONAL SCHOOL OF MOVIE CRAFTS AND ARTS

*Know All Men by These Presents that
the bearer hereof*
JOE PASTERNAK
is hereby and herewith graduated
SUMMA CUM LAUDE
*and is now entitled to Star in
Motion Pictures*

We didn't have much of a graduation, unfortunately. My teachers hated to see me go, but I was so anxious to start competing with Larry Semon that I left them no alternative but to give me the diploma I had worked so hard for. In the cafeteria, I mean, of course.

I wrote my Uncle Geza in Philadelphia who had not heard from me in months:

Dear Uncle Geza,
   I think you will be interested in knowing that by the time you read this I will be starting a new career. Since I left you I have been washing dishes, working as a busboy, doing all kinds of work while I made up my mind what my real career would be. I do not want to tell you too much, but I have graduated from a school. My teachers thought so much of me they wanted me to stay on as a scholar. But I am anxious to get started. I will tell you this. In my chosen field it is nothing for a man to make a hundred or two hundred dollars a week. Isn't this better than working in a belt factory?

And so I went to Astoria, in Queens, where I knew that Paramount Pictures had its Eastern studios.

My shoes had four coats of polish; I sat lightly all the way lest my suit get rumpled. My hat was newly blocked and cleaned. I tied a wide navy-blue ribbon around my diploma and carried it in a carefree manner under my arm.

Everybody knows what the outside of a motion picture studio looks like. Usually a high brick wall surrounds it and there is an imposing iron gate before which stand a number of policemen. It looks for all the world like a prison, except that a prison is somewhat easier to get into. Paramount's Eastern studio was no different. I walked up boldly, and the following scene took place:

ME: Are you the head guard? I wish to speak to the head guard. (I had read enough fan magazines so that I knew that the mark of a great star was that he never bothered with underlings.)

GUARD: I'm on duty here, sonny. What can I do for you?

ME (not liking that he called me "sonny"): Is the president in?

GUARD: You mean President Harding?

ME (laughing): Of course not. The president of the *studio*.

GUARD: He happens to be in Hollywood. Can I help you?

ME: I think not.

GUARD: What is it about, sonny?

ME (deciding I had no alternative but to take this man into my confidence; besides, he had a kind face): It's about my starring in the movies. You see, I've just graduated—with honors, it says so right there—and I thought I'd give you people the first break.

GUARD: That's very decent of you.

ME (with a worldly chuckle): I'm not going to try to replace Thomas Meighan or Rudolph Valentino, or anybody like that. I'm more the comedian type.

The guard took my diploma and was studying it very carefully, looking up from it now and again to eye me carefully. I began to be worried because he wasn't opening the gate for me. He muttered, "I don't know about this"; and, "I sure don't know what to tell you to do."

People who believe that the dramatic coincidence went out of fashion with the novels of Thomas Hardy and Charles Dickens, or who think it never happens in life, will have to accept this at face value, but at that moment we both turned when we heard a commotion down the street about a hundred feet from the gate. Someone was being forcibly ejected from one of the doors fronting the street. A moment later, his hat and coat were tossed into the street after him.

We both watched this, silently, for a moment. Then the guard turned back to me. "You've been gypped, kid."

"I know it," I said. "I knew it all the time, really."

"Why did you let them take you?"

"I wanted to believe them. Besides, I enjoyed it while it lasted."

He put his arm around me in a fatherly way. "What did you do before you became a movie star?"

"I was a busboy and a dishwasher."

His eyes lit up. "You don't say? You see that door down there where that fellow was just thrown out?"

"Yes."

"That's the kitchen entrance to the commissary."

"Yes?"

"And that fellow was the dishwasher."

"Yes, sir," I said, somewhat more eagerly. I was beginning to catch on.

"It happens that we're full up on movie stars out here, but I'll bet they could use a good dishwasher right now."

"I'm a *great* dishwasher."

"I'll bet you are. I'll let you into the kitchen. After that you're on your own."

"Just so long as they've got dirty dishes."

He let me in the back door. The noontime rush was at its height. I took off my coat, rolled up my sleeves, and started on a mountain of dishes. No one seemed to know who I was, or to care. I kept at the dishes for a couple

62

of hours. No sooner would the stack go down than the busboys brought in more trays.

Suddenly it was quiet. I felt someone behind me. I turned. It was a tall, strong-looking man and the way he looked at me told me a good deal about the exit of the fellow I'd seen tossed out earlier that afternoon.

"Who are you?" he demanded.

"I'm the dishwasher," I told him.

"Who hired you?"

"No one."

It took him a long time to speak again. He picked up some of the dishes I'd washed. "I'm a good dishwasher," I explained. "Lots of experience."

"Not bad," he said, putting the dishes down. "Come here."

I followed him out of the kitchen, through two swinging doors. "Have you eaten?" he asked me.

"No, sir."

"Sit down." I looked around. The Paramount Commissary—*their* dining room. Framed pictures of the movie great were all around me. I saw photographs of Gloria Swanson and Bebe Daniels and Nita Naldi and Thomas Meighan and Rudolph Valentino.

"Here?" I said breathlessly.

"Why not?"

He gestured to a waiter to bring me something to eat. "The pay's twenty dollars. And meals."

"Yes, sir," I said.

"And after you do the dishes you have to sweep up the floor."

"This floor?"

63

"Sure, this floor. What floor do you think? Is that all right?"

"Oh, yes, sir!" I said. "It'll be just fine!" I meant it from the bottom of my heart. Maybe I wouldn't be a movie star, but at least I could clean up after them, and that was good enough for me. For a start, I mean.

9. "I Picked Him"

In the Bronx, where I was living when I went to work at the Paramount Studios in Long Island as a dishwasher, they knew about my ambition to be a comedian like Larry Semon. I had a furnished room in a railroad flat with a family who still insisted on regarding me as an immigrant babe in the woods. They knew that I had enrolled in a school which had promised to make a movie star of me. In the Bronx, of course, all things are possible and while they did not exactly say they doubted what my teachers promised, they regarded my progress with a cold, fishy eye. They watched me "practice" before the bureau mirror; it impressed them, but they were still sure I was riding for a fall.

When I announced that I had presented myself at Paramount and had been put to work, skepticism turned to pride. Over dark areaways, up and down the dumbwaiters as the nightly garbage was lowered to the janitor in the cellar, the word was passed that the young man in Number 4 was working with Gloria Swanson, Bebe Daniels, and Thomas Meighan.

I tried to carry it off casually. I did not see the movie

great, being stationed before a tub of scalding water while they were lunching, but I knew enough about their eating habits to be able to spice my conversation about the movie great to everybody's satisfaction in the Bronx. The only real complication came in the matter of my dress. A man in my position could not leave for work in clothes suitable for dishwashing; and in the kitchen of the Paramount commissary, they were always astonished by my wardrobe. I wore a felt hat, a stickpin in my tie, and showed a confident amount of handkerchief at the breast pocket. It meant changing to work clothes before I got to the sink, but it was the only way out.

One day, about a month after I'd started wrestling with the dishes, one of the busboys failed to show up for work.

"Do you mind, Joe?" the manager asked me. His name was Bill Williams and he was the same big, formidable man who found me washing dishes and hired me. He and his wife had taken me under their wing.

Did I mind? The dining room was sacred ground to me. I swept it every day, feeling myself privileged. I knew which was Gloria Swanson's table and where the directors sat. I assured Williams that I would consider it an honor. Contact with the movie great (or should I say, contact with their dirty dishes) had only made me more movie-struck.

The first thing I saw was Nita Naldi, sheathed in shiny black sequins, holding court at her table. She took her movie characterizations very literally—a thing that often happens—and she flashed her long, bare arms, encircled with diamonds and rings, just as if she were some Roman empress teasing her lovers. I was enthralled. My stack of

66

dishes was within good view of her and I kept piling it high with my eyes fixed on her.

Finally I lifted it up and was making my way to the kitchen when, large as life, standing right before me and smiling at me as though he knew me, I saw the star of *The Miracle Man,* Thomas Meighan. Our eyes met, mine glazed with awe, unable to return the smile.

I dropped the tray of dishes all over him.

Williams came rushing up to us. I had liberally stained the great star with coffee dregs, gravy, and soup. Williams apologized to Meighan and gave me a killing look. "It was my fault, Bill," Tom said, "I tripped him." He winked at me knowingly. "Sorry, kid."

After that I stopped staring at the actors and began to realize they were people.

I never dropped another dish and when one of the waiters left, Williams and his wife let me wait on tables. In the Bronx, when I showed them my new tuxedo, they were very impressed. "Adolphe Menjou better watch out," someone called to me across the hall.

My first tables were among the members of the working crew: the assistant directors, operating cameramen, prop men, and so on. The money was good, better than I imagined, but I had my heart set on serving the actors. The other waiters told me I was crazy. Actors were temperamental; they couldn't be pleased, no matter how hard you tried. If it wasn't too hot, it was too cold. And if it was just right, it was too tough or too mushy. As for the bigger tips they gave, it wasn't worth the trouble.

I arranged to buy another waiter's station by promising him a share of the tips I would make for a month. "It's like taking candy from a baby," he said. "You sure you want to do it?"

But his station included Gloria Swanson's table and I wanted to be her waiter more than anything in the world. I used to steal glances at her while I was wrestling with the dirty dishes. But as her waiter she would actually talk to me. Gloria Swanson was the perfect star: she played the part away from the camera as well as before it. She had the shine that marks a true star. Many affect it, some hopelessly. But there are just a very few that the people in the world of show business know as really great personalities. Swanson was one of these. As a waiter, I could think of nothing more wonderful than to be *her* waiter.

From the waiter's point of view, she was magnificent. She was regal, she was self-possessed, and she demanded perfect service. I shook and quaked as she talked to me, but I knew how to win her heart. She liked her salad greens cold and crisp. So I spread some of my tip money around the kitchen to make sure she got what she liked. Soon she was telling other actors about me and it became a mark of distinction for a lesser player to have *her* waiter. I arranged the Swanson diet, told her what to order and shook my head if she asked for something that had not appealed to me in the kitchen.

The one fear that gripped me was that once, as I would be serving her—an act which sometimes brought my cheek frighteningly close to hers—she would turn to look at me. I felt sure that if she ever did this, I would drop whatever I was serving right in her lap. And if I did again to her what I had done to Tom Meighan, I was afraid what the management would do to me.

68

The high spot in my career as a waiter came one evening when Rudolph Valentino, another one of my customers on Gloria's recommendation, asked me if I would be good enough to deliver a package for him to a friend on my way home. The friend lived on Riverside Drive. I could have the Valentino basket-weave Rolls-Royce limousine and the liveried chauffeur.

We drove to the Bronx first, me rattling around in back, and loving every minute and every stare. I was offhand about the car, assured everybody that it was Rudy's car but that he had let me have it for the evening. Owning the car would not have impressed them in the Bronx as much as being on such friendly terms with the great Valentino that he gave me his limousine. "See you later. I've got to see a man on Riverside Drive." I tried to be offhand about it, for the Drive was considered a fashionable street in our world.

My double life almost came to an end when a young reporter whose beat was the movies and the studios did a piece about me for a New York paper. The reporter was Richard Watts, Jr.; I remember that he called it "Smiling Joe" and he made a flat prediction. "This boy won't be a waiter long," Dick said.

How he was able to read my mind I cannot explain to this day. Maybe Dick thought I still had my heart set on being an actor, for it was an open secret around the dining room that I had come to the studio in the first place to be an actor. Every so often someone would kid me about it; the assistant directors particularly liked to say they needed someone just like me and then own up that they were just stringing me along.

69

But I wasn't sure I wanted to be an actor any more. I had even come to the conclusion that waiting on them might be a dead, if profitable, end. Acting folk were glamorous, they were fun, they were handsome and beautiful, but that was all.

I arranged to trade sections with a waiter during a time when some of the actors who liked me were out of town. I wanted to wait on the directors. I had learned that while an actor may think the world of you, it is the director who actually makes the picture, who can promote or demote. This trade also involved my paying for the new station, but I had no doubt it was a good move. I waited on Gregory La Cava, Allan Dwan, Irving Willard, and Herbert Brenon, among others. I grew to like them all and to respect them. But the one I was really drawn to at once was Allan Dwan. I picked him.

Allan was an impressive figure of a man, intensely serious, single-minded and single-purposed. He lived motion pictures and regarded everything that did not concern the making of exposed film as an intrusion. He was a cantankerous customer for a waiter. Nothing was ever right and when he was handed a menu, there was so much to choose from that he ended up not being able to make up his mind at all. I noticed that he tore into rolls, picked at the bread and hardly ate any of it.

When I found out what he liked, I stopped giving him the menu. He would come in, followed by the people with whom he was working on the set, talking pictures, the last shot, or the first shot to be made after the lunch break. I'd have ready for him something he'd once eaten with some relish. At first he looked at me darkly, with a who-

the-devil-told-you-to-bring-this look. Then he realized that
he could go on talking shop without having to think about
food, and he appeared to be grateful. Once I gave him
the menu, just to be sure.

"You know what I want, Joe," he told me. That was
all I needed to know.

Since he didn't like the bread and rolls provided by
the commissary, I took to picking up a loaf of a seeded
Russian rye such as you could buy at any corner in the
Bronx. I'd slice it, put it before him, and was always
astonished to see how much he relished it. I was sick for
a couple of days once and another waiter had to take my
place. Allan was prepared to put up with that, but he
called over George Williams and asked why in good-grief
he couldn't have his usual bread.

"What bread?" Williams asked.

"That good rye bread, of course," Dwan exploded. "Do
I have to waste a whole hour describing a miserable loaf
of bread to you?"

They brought out everything in the kitchen, but they
could not find anything that resembled Allan's favorite.
As soon as I returned, they asked me about it. I told Allan
what I had been doing.

"Why'd you do that, son?" Dwan asked me.

"Why not? You like it, don't you?"

Some time after this Dwan was making a Foreign Legion
picture with Ben Lyon. While I was serving them I overheard, as always, their current problems. It seemed that
on the next day they would have to shoot a close-up of
one of the legionnaires. They already had a long shot of
the soldiers marching out of the desert fortress, going off

across the hot sands to what would be glorious extinction. Left behind was one legionnaire who had fallen ill and was unable to go into battle with his buddies. Wan and pale, he would lift himself to the hospital window and look out at the column of men marching away. He would begin to weep, first slowly, then piteously.

"What we need," one of the assistants said, "is someone with a corn-fed look, kind of wide-eyed and naïve. Someone who can turn those tears on and off."

I felt as though a million volts had been shot through my body. Hadn't I been able to weep whole oceans for those racketeers? And that sick soldier they described—why couldn't he look like me?

I took the assistant aside. I couldn't be sure whether they were kidding me again, as they had so often in the past. But they let me discuss it with Dwan and he was not the kind to waste time on practical jokes.

"How about me?" I said.

"You for what?"

"For that shot tomorrow. The soldier, crying." I told him about my experience.

Dwan looked at me carefully. Then he grinned. "Okay," he said crisply. "Tomorrow."

Mine was to be the first shot in the morning. I was in makeup at dawn and ready to work before the crew had arrived. Allan explained the situation to me again, the sick soldier who hears the singing of his buddies as they go out to face extinction. It sounded beautifully sad to me.

"All right, let's rehearse it," Dwan suggested.

The rehearsals didn't go so well, but Dwan was not

disturbed. "It's better. I don't want to get a performance out of you when we're not rolling. Save yourself."

Finally he called, "Roll 'em," and we were ready for the first take.

I couldn't make the tears come.

"All right, cut," someone called. No one was flustered, or worried. It isn't easy to cry, they realized.

"Try it again," Allan said. The camera started to turn; Allan called for me to break out into tears.

Nothing.

"You feel all right, Joe?" the assistant asked me. "Not nervous or anything?"

"Oh, no. I'm all right." I told him how sometimes I could cry three times during one lunch hour.

"Sure. Do it now for us, will you, kid? This scene is holding up the whole picture."

"All right. Let's go," I said.

"Here we go," called the assistant. "Roll 'em."

Still no tears.

I could see the director and assistants exchange glances. But Dwan came up to me, walking slowly. "Save the lights," he ordered. He put his arm around me. I knew he liked me and he wanted me to succeed. "Anything I can do for you? Is there any music that makes you sad? I can bring over the studio musicians for a little mood music if it'd help you, Joe."

He made me feel there was no pressure, no rush, that he was my friend, that he was pulling for me, that I could take as long as I liked.

"Hit 'em all," the assistant called. The stage lights went on. The camera started to turn again.

73

No tears.

It went that way until lunch. Dwan wasn't troubled, or if he was, he certainly did not let on to me. "We'll get it after lunch, son. Don't worry."

All afternoon they rubbed my cheeks with fresh onions, dropped glycerine in my eyes, blew smoke into them. And still no tears. I could not understand it myself. I was shaken with the consequences of what I was doing to myself; I prayed, I begged myself to relax, or to tense up, or whatever I used to be able to do to make the tears flow like water. But not even all the backstage tricks of the stage crew could moisten my eyes.

Finally Dwan called a merciful halt. "All right, boys, that'll do it for today."

They let me stand by the window, looking out. No one said anything to me. The stage lights went out. The director and his assistants left.

I sat down on the cot and started to weep, shaking with great, racking sobs that came from the soles of my feet. I cried at my lack of talent, at my stupidity, my brass at thinking I could be an actor. I wept for the shame of taking advantage of Allan Dwan. I wept for the life I had thrown aside, as "Smiling Joe" in the Paramount commissary.

But I wept alone, for there was no one on the stage to see me.

I don't know how long I stayed there. Later—it seemed to me much later—someone came up to me. "Mr. Dwan wants to see you," he said coldly.

I sucked in my breath and went to face the music. Dwan

was in his office; his face wore a look of annoyance that comes from a thoroughly wasted day.

"Sit down," he said, jutting a thumb to a chair. He waited until we were alone. "Well," he began, "as an actor you *are* lousy. Do you have any doubts about that?"

I shook my head. I nodded. I meant I agreed with him.

"I was happy to give you a chance. I'd do it again, not for you, maybe, but for someone who's done what you've done. I've had my eye on you, you know that?" I shook my head. My eyes, for some reason I could not understand, were beginning to be wet with tears. "You work hard, you've got spunk, drive, initiative. So you're a terrible actor—is that a crime? So you didn't want to be a waiter all your life—is that a crime?"

Then he turned to his desk and scratched a name on a piece of paper. "I want you to see this man tomorrow morning. I think you belong in this business. We've got enough loafers and lobby-guys. We need some people like you. You're going to work for me. I'm making you my chairman."

I didn't know what a chairman was. He made it sound like two distinct syllables, *chair-man*, but I had always thought a chairman had something to do with running a company.

The next morning I found out what my duties as chairman involved. Mr. Dwan had a number of canvas chairs, of different height. One was his close-up chair, another was his medium-shot chair, his long-shot chair—and so on, I think there were eight in all. My duties consisted of seeing that as the shots were completed and the new ones readied, Mr. Dwan's proper chair was waiting for him.

75

As a waiter I had been making between eighty and a hundred and twenty-five dollars a week, depending on my tips. As Allan Dwan's chairman, my salary was a flat twenty-five dollars a week. But my check was made out by Paramount Pictures and it was vouchered by the Production Department. My title was "Third Assistant Director." I was the happiest man in the world.

10. W. C. Fields, the Marquise and a Girl Named Mary

I AM not a sociologist but I would like an expert in such things to tell me just when the fun went out of earning a living. My own theory is that it began when the country started to be peopled with a new professional group called accountants. Now, I have nothing against accountants and it may be that if we didn't have them, we'd have to invent them. When the income tax began, it was inevitable that more careful records would have to be kept. More careful records, accountants—and there we are.

It may seem strange for a producer of motion pictures, who is usually caricatured as screaming because someone is squandering his money, to complain about a plague of accountants. Blame it on my nostalgia for freer, happier days. Our business practices in the old days would be sure to give the Department of the Treasury and the firm of Price, Waterhouse & Company the galloping conniptions, but we had a good time while it lasted.

It was nothing for us to work all day and all night because there wasn't anything else that was as much fun as making pictures. We broke the rules, we took advantage of

77

a lot of good-natured people, but, in the end, everybody laughed.

Back in the early Twenties, even a Third Assistant Director, or keeper of the chairs, felt that there was no job in the world quite like his. I must have shown some marked ability about having the right chair in the right place when Mr. Dwan wanted to sit down, because within a year he promoted me to Second Assistant Director. Though the title sounded impressive in the Bronx, I knew that a Third Assistant bore the same relationship to a director that a ditch-digger bears to an engineer, the ditch-digger being the Third Assistant Engineer.

But a Second Assistant? He was there. He carried out the assistant's orders and the assistant got *his* from the director. "We need forty extras tomorrow. Twenty blondes and brunettes. All pretty. . . . Order about five hundred dollars' worth of flowers for that wedding scene, Joe. . . . The boss saw a picture of General and Mrs. Vanderbilt going to the opera. See if we can get a chinchilla wrap just like the one she wore."

Maybe I had too much fun in my job. I know that after washing dishes or hustling them from kitchen to dining room and back as busboy and waiter, anything having to do with motion pictures didn't seem to me like work. I loved it.

Once, on location in Florida during the boom there, a big real estate promoter approached me and offered me five times what Paramount was paying me. "And that isn't all," he said. "With what you'll learn being around me, you'll be able to take that money and triple it."

"What would I have to do?" I inquired.

"We'll buy land, subdivide, sell it. I guarantee you'll be retired before you're thirty."

He was no fly-by-night promoter; I found that out. His offer was genuine. I turned it down, to his amazement. "But why?" he asked me. "Didn't I offer you enough money? Maybe I can give you more." I told him that the only trouble was: I wouldn't have any fun in his line of business.

Maybe a fellow can take much too much pleasure in his work. I used to be kidded mercilessly by some of the older hands on the set. Once I was sent to Yonkers to get a "film-stretcher" because, I was told, our picture had turned out to be too short and we had to stretch every frame of every picture to make it come out the right length. I was sent to a paint factory to get some black white paint, that being a color which would be used in a night shot without showing. I always went. You wouldn't believe what a trusting guy I was.

I made other trips and errands out into the world for left-handed wrenches, invisible electric bulbs, upside-down hammers, and other absurdities it pains me to have to recall. I always knew there was a chance something was being pulled on me, but my feeling was that maybe, *maybe* there was such a thing as a film-stretcher, and the best way to find out was to look for it.

Besides, I was used to being asked in dead earnest to find the most outlandish things. Once we needed a tattooed countess, a real countess. I found one. I had to find shoes that would melt when they touched water; water that would turn to gelatine, and a beautiful yacht that would sink immediately it was launched. You can't blame me for thinking an upside-down hammer might exist.

Today, in our age of accountants, there is little room even for the harmless practical joke. I'd have to sign out, sign in, fill in forms, explain to some sober keeper of the records what my mission was, and why: all of which would be duly recorded, the costs analyzed by somebody with no sense of humor—it's impossible.

This whole attitude is reflected also in our actors. Our players were fascinating people in those days. Maybe you would not have voted them into the Senate but they gave our national life a color it hasn't had since the acting profession fell into the hands of the professional business manager, who is really only an accountant who works for you, anyway.

I remember W. C. Fields, the last of the great and unreconstructed individualists. When I was working as an assistant director on one of his pictures, a silent film we shot in Florida, I thought the way Bill Fields carried on was shocking. (I had the intolerance usual in youth.) Later on, I grew to know him well. I then realized that he was a great clown, that his contempt for authority was necessary for his style. He flouted the rules because he was a lonely man who liked being alone and didn't want to be bothered with anybody or anything. This was as true about the rules of billiards as it was about driving.

Our picture was shot on the Stotesbury estate at Palm Beach. How or why they ever gave us permission to use their magnificent lawns and fabulous gardens, I will never know. I had charge of the details and, of course, I was met by a half dozen high-ranking butlers who begged me to understand that the Florida sun was very hard on grass and to be sure to see that each blade was handled with the utmost of care.

I assured them that we were all lovers of grass; we wouldn't dream of stepping too hard on their priceless lawns. When we were ready for shooting, the camera picked up Bill Fields in a tin lizzie turning into the road that led to the Stotesbury house. The car was supposed to wheel dangerously close to the shoulder of the road and brush a hedge. The butlers threw up their hands in horror at the first take. I assured them that what they saw was not in the script and would not happen again.

I went to Fields between shots and explained the extreme distress that his driving had caused among the Stotesbury help. I explained our responsibilities, our profound obligation for being permitted to shoot a picture on the magnificent estate and our gratitude for their generosity.

"Sure, kid, sure. I understand," Fields said.

I went back to the servants to quiet them down. I could see Fields talking hard to Eddie Sutherland, our director, but of course I did not know what they were talking about.

On the second take, Bill left the road entirely, plowed clear through the hedge, trailed across the lawn, up and down and around, the wheels of the Ford digging deep trenches in the carefully tended turf. Sutherland was pleased. "Wonderful, Bill! It's uproarious!" he exclaimed. "Let's do it again, even wilder this time, Bill!"

I took refuge from the irate posse of butlers in some nearby shrubbery.

Of course Bill Fields was a great enough comedian to

81

realize that precisely because it *was* the Stotesbury estate, it would be funny if he made a hash of their lawns. He certainly would not have thought of it if I had not brought to his attention a beautiful way to flout authority, even the authority of the Stotesbury butlers.

But not all our players wanted to make fun of the aristocracy. When Gloria Swanson married Henri de la Falaise de la Coudray, a real marquis, it was obvious that our Gloria was going to be a changed woman. Having been her waiter, my relationship with her was on an extremely informal basis. I had never found her temperamental. The stories I had heard about the battle royal between the two reigning Paramount queens, Pola Negri and Gloria Swanson, were just stories to me. (We heard that Gloria loathed cats and Negri loved them. When Negri was brought to the Paramount lot in Hollywood, she insisted on having cats all over the place. This deeply offended Gloria, who refused to have them near her. The Paramount executives only solved this dilemma by sending Gloria to the New York studios where she could reign undisturbed by felines.)

But after her marriage, Gloria became very conscious of her rights and privileges. She informed the crew that henceforth she no longer wished to be called "Gloria," or "Miss Swanson," as we had been doing. She was to be addressed as "the Marquise," or better, "Madame la Marquise." It came a little easier to me, perhaps, with my European background, but people like the operating cameramen had a terrible time. They had been used to saying things like: "Hey, Gloria, would you move over just a bit to the left? That's it, honey, stand right there." Now they had to change all this to: "Would the Marquise be kind enough, please, to move slightly to her left?"

It is my belief, of course, that a good deal of this kind of thing was expected of our stars in what has been called the era of wonderful nonsense. We'd have been disappointed if our movie stars had behaved less regally. Today we are accustomed to seeing our glamor girls making apple popovers in the kitchen or wheeling a basket in a supermarket. In those days such things would have been unthinkable. A star's greatness was often measured in direct proportion to the outlandish tastes and demands we had to fulfill for her.

One blistering hot day—and of course there was no such thing as an air-conditioned stage then—Gloria, I mean the Marquise, had us bring several hundred pounds of ice to the edge of the stage. We mounted a brace of fans behind them and wafted cool, if damp, breezes at her as our star emoted.

On another occasion, Gloria was distressed by the commotion being made by Madge Kennedy, who was playing a scene right next to her own set. (In the days of silent pictures three and four pictures were often shot on the same stage, right alongside each other.) Finally, Gloria sent word to the neighboring company that she would not be able to work unless there was less noise from the next set.

An assistant director returned to explain that Miss Kennedy was playing a scene in which she was being violently abducted and that the script called for her to scream for help.

"Very well," said Gloria, all Marquise, "but will you ask her, please, to scream more quietly?"

Often I was most surprised to find that the stars with the greatest reputation for temperament were the most tractable. For instance, Rudolph Valentino. He proved, as far as I was concerned, to be quiet, sedate, submissive, almost *bourgeois*. I knew his reputation. He had been a leading man for years. As early as 1919 he had had top billing in *A Society Sensation* with Carmel Myers.

Then in 1921 he had made *The Four Horsemen of the Apocalypse* with Rex Ingram directing for the old Metro company. The picture skyrocketed Valentino to the very top of the movie world. But he proved to be so difficult— so the story ran, in any case—that he was released. With which Valentino went over to Paramount, only to make *The Sheik* and prove to be a bigger star than ever.

But even there (on the West Coast) he was to prove troublesome. He was married to an adopted daughter of Richard Hudnut, the cosmetics man, who billed herself as Natasha Rambova. For several years they toured the country as a dance team, mainly, I suppose, because Rudy was supposed to be too difficult for any studio to handle.

But when he came to Paramount's Long Island studio I could not imagine what all the fuss was about. He was sweet, almost shy. When I called him, he arrived on the set, ready to work. The fact is, I never met a more cooperative actor than Rudy. It only goes to show.

But it was not the big, the famous players who caught my eye. It was an unknown, timid beginner who almost changed my whole life. For reasons which shall be presently clear, I shall call her Mary Hilton, which wasn't her

name at all. I met her while driving out of the studio
one night in Allan Dwan's town car. I was running some
errand for him and using his car and chauffeur. I had to
stop at the gate for a moment and there I saw Mary
Hilton. She was petite, charming, and so pretty that I
forgot what my errand was. She had worked in my picture
that day and she knew who I was, so she smiled. I returned
the smile. And of course:

"May I give you a lift home?"

"Oh, would you, Mr. Pasternak?" she said, her voice
thrilled.

I played the grand man. It was nothing at all, I was
delighted, and all the rest of it.

All the way into Manhattan she told me of her ambition
to be a film star. Her family had other plans for her, but
she had her own idea of what she wanted to do with her
life. I had met many girls since my arrival in America,
but none of them hit me the way Mary Hilton did. I could
not quite understand it. She struck me as being a very
lonely, lost girl; she had a gamin quality to her. I pictured her living in a tenement with a family that beat
her every time she spoke of being an actress.

I asked her where we could drop her. She hesitated for
a moment. "At the next subway stop." We were at Lexington Avenue and Seventy-ninth. I told her we could
let her off at her door, if she liked. She didn't think that
was a good idea.

"I'd like to see you again," I said.

"I would too," she said.

"Tomorrow?"

She nodded.

85

"What's your address?"

She swallowed hard. "I'll meet you here. Right at this entrance."

I didn't like the idea, but I thought it must be because of her family, so I said all right, we'd meet at the corner. I watched her walk down the street and then rapped on the glass and told the chauffeur to get going.

I had not forgotten about Rosika, back in my home town. Though I did not write her, I still had no doubt that one day I would return and make her mine. I often thought of her, just as I often thought of my village. I loved my new country intensely, but I had to confess that my theory that no place I had seen, no girl I had seen, was half so beautiful as my town, or Rosika, was having a hard time surviving. Yet I kept it alive.

I was completely taken by Mary. It may have come from the air of intrigue that surrounded her. I was never permitted to bring her home, to see her to the door, to telephone her. Still she always desperately wanted to see me. As I grew to know her better, I tried to let her know the truth about the importance of my position as a Second Assistant Director. Since I had been Allan Dwan's chairman, I had become sufficiently sophisticated in the way of the movie world not to overestimate my own position. Besides, I liked Mary enough so that I did not want ever to be accused of misleading her in the slightest.

But she had unbounded faith in me. My protestations she took as evidence of my modesty. She said she didn't care, that she knew I would go far, that she believed in me. So every night I pictured her going home to her family's cold-water flat, way over on the East Side, and

86

stretching her tired limbs out on her bed and gazing at a water-stained ceiling. The jobs as a movie extra that I was able to throw in her direction were her only contact with the great, glamorous world outside her slum. No wonder she believed in me.

We were to leave, Allan Dwan, Gloria Swanson, and the rest of us, to make a picture which would be shot, mostly, on location at New Martinsville, Georgia. We would need sixty girls and, needless to say, I invited Mary to be part of the company. But it was impossible. Her family absolutely forbade it and she could not dare to go without their permission.

New Martinsville turned out to be quite an experience in my life. Prohibition had fallen over the country. Dwan's First Assistant, and several others in the company, discovered that corn likker could be bought from a number of the locals. Result: one morning Dwan had no First Assistant. Always precise, businesslike, Allan would not stand for this nonsense. He promoted me to First Assistant on the spot.

I worked harder than ever. In fact, we did so well that I was able to pare three days off our out-of-town schedule. A saving like this is always most welcome to production executives, for every day a company shoots, especially on location, is an added expense.

We arrived back in New York with a suitable fanfare. Dwan was generous in my behalf, telling everyone how I had taken charge, how I had been able to speed production, and how invaluable I had proved. I expected a bonus.

Sure enough, bright and early the next morning, after

I had arranged for the company to finish its final scenes on the lot, I was called for. "Good luck," Allan said, with a knowing wink. "Don't just take a bonus. Make 'em give you a raise too. Tell them I insist on it."

But when I walked into the executive's office, he didn't even ask me to sit down. "You're through," he said. "Pick up what's coming to you and get off the lot."

There was no discussion, no reason.

I went back to Dwan. "Mr. Dwan," I said, "I've been fired."

"You've been *what?*" He couldn't believe it either.

"Fired."

He got to his feet angrily. "There must be a mistake. They can't do that to you, not after what you've done around this place. Wait here."

I waited.

He returned, looking very pale, I thought. "That's it, Joe," he said.

"But why? What have I done?"

He shook his head. "I don't know. They just don't want you around here any more."

"But why?" I was frantic. "What have I done?"

"They say they're going to close the studio anyway."

"I can't believe that. It's something else, what?"

"I've told you, Joe, that's what they said. Something happened on location."

"But what? Do you think they believe I wasn't honest?"

"It wasn't that. That much I know. Let's let it go at that, shall we?"

All I can say, across the years, is that I still don't know and I hope Allan will tell me one day just why I was fired.

88

I didn't tell anyone what had happened. There was a message from Mary Hilton to call her. I didn't feel much like talking to anyone, but I called her just the same. What was I doing? Could I see her? She sounded eager to see me. "I've made an important decision. What are you doing this afternoon? Will you take me to lunch?"

I said I would. She looked lovely. For some reason she didn't seem so troubled, so depressed, so hemmed in by her world. "I've made up my mind not to be an actress," she said. "I wasn't fitted for it, and I don't think I'd have been very good at it anyway."

"You'll be happier this way," I said. "It's a very heart-breaking business. They love you one day and the next no one will give you the time of day."

"Aren't you glad I've decided to quit?"

Under the circumstances, I could control my enthusiasm, but I tried to smile anyway.

"I want you to come to my house tonight," she insisted.

"Is it all right? They won't mind?"

"You must. Will you promise to come?" I said I would. And she gave me the address. I was surprised, to say the least, but not as surprised as when I presented myself at the door of a Fifth Avenue apartment building later that evening, was escorted to the elevator, and whisked up to the top floor. Once inside, an establishment of Gothic proportions, Mary came up to me, linked her arm in mine, and walked me among her guests. Every last one of them was a name out of the society columns. As for Mary, it came to me that her family name was that of one of this country's biggest independent oil operators. And, of course, that was why she hadn't asked me home;

89

but now that she had yielded to her family and given up this nonsense of wanting to be in the movies, she could lead her own life.

I left quickly. I didn't want to be introduced as "the great foreign film director," or even to talk to Mary, not now, after I was fired. She found me the next day. "I want to marry you," she said. Had I not been fired, I'd have forgotten about Rosika, I do believe, but I told her the truth. I would be without a job in a few weeks, I had no prospects, little future.

"I'll marry you anyway."

"I couldn't afford you."

"What are you going to do?"

"I'm going to California," I said. "I have no alternative."

"I'll write you, my darling," she said. "Every day. So you won't forget me."

But I knew I would. I don't know why, for I had thought I was very much in love with her. But my world had collapsed, without warning and it seemed to me without justice, and once again I was on the move. Who cared about love?

11. California

On May 21, 1926, I became a citizen of the United States.

These simple words cannot convey what I felt when I stood up before a judge in Foley Square, New York, and took the oath of allegiance. Quite simply I'd like to say this. Every so often one reads a statement by some two-bit patriot who makes it appear that no one quite belongs in our country who hasn't got three generations behind him here. I won't argue the proposition now. But I'll amend it to this extent. No one can love this country like an immigrant.

I was unemployed. My prospects were dim. I was advised against going out to Hollywood where, I was told, jobs were few and far between. But I had never been so elated. I waited in New York only long enough to get my citizenship papers before I left for California.

I could afford an upper berth, I remember that, yet most of the nights I sat up, in the men's dressing room, lighting cigarette after cigarette, looking out at the endless American plain. I had done a good deal of traveling with our companies that went on location. I had come to know the South. But this was the first time I discovered

America as an American. I could not sleep. I was like a man who has come across an enormous wealth which no one can ever take away from him. *It's mine,* I kept saying to myself, *I belong, I'm part of it.* Maybe I should have been worried about being out of work; I preferred to take stock of my assets. I had saved a little money. My insurance was paid up for a year or so in advance. Out in Hollywood were a number of directors with whom I'd worked on Long Island. And I was an American.

Hollywood at that time was making the transition from orange groves and end-of-the-streetcar-line to a kind of sun-drenched business community. The pepper and eucalyptus trees along Hollywood Boulevard had been chopped down, despite the public pleas by Mary Pickford and the Save-Our-Trees Committee. Hollywood Boulevard itself still had a number of private homes alongside the new buildings that were going up. The other streets were mostly unpaved. Little Spanish bungalows stood next to older frame houses, all corners and gingerbread.

I took a room right next to the Paramount Studio on Marathon Street. Bright and early my first morning I went to see my friends from New York. I tried not to give the impression that I needed a job urgently. I was just "looking around," I told them. I was considering making my home out here. No one was particularly encouraging, but I let them know that I was planning to stay anyway.

The act I was putting on became transparent as time wore on. If I was merely surveying the ground, as I'd been saying, I'd have returned long since. But I stayed on because I had no alternative. My money went faster than

I'd anticipated. I decided to stop playing coy and lay it on the line about needing a job.

I dropped in on Eddie Sutherland, with whom I'd worked back East. "I'd like to, Joe," he said, and I knew he wasn't giving me the old business, "but I can't. I've got an assistant out here. He's a good boy, works hard. You wouldn't want me to fire him, would you?"

"No, Eddie. Of course not."

"Cheer up. You'll make a connection. Something's bound to turn up."

There was a little restaurant across the street from the studio and I went in for a cup of coffee. There, with a Coca-Cola in one hand and a Piedmont cigarette curling smoke in the other, I saw Billy Wilkerson.

Today W. R. Wilkerson is the publisher of the *Hollywood Reporter*, the motion picture trade paper which is as indispensable to the industry as raw film stock and theatres. I met him first in my New York days when I was waiting on tables. Billy had been a film salesman. I liked him when I first met him and I've never ceased loving him, though we have had our differences on this and that.

He looked then as he looks now, carefully tailored, his mustache waxed, and with the inevitable coke and Piedmont near his hands. He has always been a perfectionist, in life as well as in love. Having achieved perfection, he loses interest. Though I lived with him, he was a mystery to me, as he has remained a mystery to me ever since. I once told him he was the most kind-hearted cruel man I ever met. If Billy wants something, nothing had better stand in his way. And yet he is a man capable of the warmest gestures, a man whose only fault (if it is a fault) is that he is always shooting for the moon, and nothing less than perfection will suffice for him.

Billy looked at me through the smoke curling from his fingers.

"Joe. What you doing here?"

I put the same question to him.

He shrugged. He was trying to make a connection. But he pressed me to answer. I told him I was trying to get a job, without much success. He looked at me for a long moment, took a pull from his coke and said suddenly: "Let's you and me move in together. We'll do something."

"What?"

"Something big. I've got an idea. Okay?"

"Okay."

"How much money you got?"

"Thirty dollars. Twenty-five, something like that."

He frowned slightly. "That's not enough. Can you get any more?"

"Eddie Sutherland offers me money every time I see him."

"You go back to see Eddie. Drink up. I'll wait here."

In fifteen minutes I had a hundred-dollar check.

"Where are you living?" Billy asked now. He shook his head at my answer. "That's a fleabag. We can't live there. I'll tell you what we do. We're going to rent an apartment. A nice one. Let's go."

Needless to say, the apartment was handsome. The day after we moved in, I heard Billy on the phone, calling about a classified ad. He was looking for a butler with flawless qualifications, a boy thoroughly experienced in serving two demanding gentlemen.

I broke in, with more nervousness than tact. "What are you doing, Billy?" I demanded. "You know we can't afford anyone like that."

"Leave everything to me," he insisted.

Back on the phone, he said: "Also put in that he's got to be reliable and able to furnish a bond of two hundred and fifty dollars."

The next day we had our choice of three Filipino boys. We chose one who not only filled the bill perfectly but asked Billy if he could just deposit with him the sum of two hundred and fifty dollars in cash as a token of his honesty. Billy allowed as to how that might be agreeable.

Later that day Billy drove up in a new car. "My God, Billy!" I exclaimed. "Where'd you get that?"

"My dear boy, haven't you heard of low down payments and the conveniences offered by installment buying? Now get your hat and come along with me. You're a big director, you understand? You've directed pictures."

"What's up?"

"Don't ask any questions. Let's go."

We drove to the Paramount lot where Billy parked the car just outside the main gate. "Wait here," he told me.

After some moments he came out with El Brendel, who will be remembered as one of the ranking comedians of the silent screen. Billy pointed grandly at me sitting in the car and said, "Here's that man I was telling you about. I want you to meet the great European director, Josef Von Pasternak."

He brought the comedian into the car so we could

95

have a conference. "Nice car you've got," Brendel said, looking about.

"Thanks."

"He's just had a fight with Paramount," Billy said of our guest. "They haven't been treating him right. I told him you might be willing to direct him in a two-reeler."

My eyes must have bugged out when I looked at Billy. We did not have enough money for next month's rent, not to mention the car payment, nor the butler's salary. To talk about making a motion picture was fantastic. Billy did not give me the chance to say a word. "I told him you'd say yes if he's willing."

Brendel was still looking at the new car. There was a little vase—automobile designers thought of everything in those days—and Billy, or our boy, had put a little rose in it. Brendel fingered it, then suddenly said: "Okay, we start Monday. You got story?"

"Of course we've got a story," Billy said, very fast, before I could utter a word. "You don't think we'd come without a story, do you?" He forced a jovial chuckle and firmly but politely eased Brendel out of the car and went back into the studio with him.

By the time Billy came out, I was ready to return to New York. I was worried about my limited experience, about our lack of money, and not least of all about what El Brendel would do when he found out what we had done to him. But Billy was undismayed. He had it all figured out.

I borrowed to the limit on my insurance policy; I wired my brother Emil, whom I had brought over from the old country a couple of years before, for what money he could

spare. Billy added what he could raise. He made a deal
for space at the old Christie Studio and arranged with a
friend to sneak our company into the back entrance to
the Lasky Ranch (now the location of the Warner Bros.
Studio) and save the fifty-dollar-a-day rental we'd have to
pay for the privilege of the front gate. Everybody worked
for a participating share. Our capital came to about six
hundred dollars in all, which was spent only for raw film
stock and extras, who then were paid at the rate of three
dollars a day.

Billy and I dreamed up a story. We called it *Help Yourself,* and what do you think it was about? A well-meaning
but clumsy lad gets a job in a cafeteria and in trying to
be helpful proceeds to make a mess of things. It was more
than faintly autobiographical.

As for the picture itself, I was astonished at the detail
a director had to keep in his mind. Though you change
your angles, your people must always make their entrances
from the proper side; cameras, performers, lights—everything is the director's province. I had worked with half
a dozen of the best directors, but given a director's chair,
I was scared to death and incompetent.

The picture showed it. I had people coming in from
the left where they'd exited from the right. I left out all
sorts of little things that rocked our heads when we looked
at the finished film for a story transition. We were in
terrible trouble; we knew it. The picture simply didn't
hang together.

"I've got a friend. He'll help us," Billy said.

He brought in Wesley Ruggles, then, as he is today,
one of the finest makers of comedy in our country. Ruggles

studied the film and groaned. He didn't have to tell us what was wrong with it. We knew. But he made a few suggestions which got us out of our difficulty, enough so Billy could sell the picture at any rate. Then Ruggles turned to me.

"Technically it's a botch," he said. "But there are some really nice things in the picture. Did you ever direct before?" I had to admit I hadn't; I told him what I'd been doing in New York. "The picture's nothing to be ashamed of. The technical stuff anybody with a sixth-grade education can learn in time. What you did in that picture was make us like the busboy. He was sympathetic. He wasn't just a name, someone running around on the film. He was a person. And you achieved some nice touches, kind of homey and likable. Most directors forget about them." He broke off abruptly. "Go and see the studio manager at Universal tomorrow and tell him I want you to be my assistant. If you don't mind," he added as an afterthought, "being an assistant again."

I must have had the look of a man who has been rescued after swimming beyond his depth, because Ruggles gave me an encouraging nudge and a wink. As for Billy, his mind was already racing on to some other venture.

12. An Interview with Laemmle

IF you came across the Universal back lot in those days, riding a horse over the Cahuenga Pass from Hollywood, you would have thought you had come to a town in the Texas cow country at the turn of the century. The only curious feature you might have noted was a lack of population and the fact that the houses, banks, saloons, stables, and sheriffs' offices were all front and no rear premises. But the streets were dusty, deep-rutted; wasps buzzed in the eaves near the Wells Fargo station; the batwing doors of the Red Dog saloon swung in the breeze. When a company was shooting, perhaps with William Wyler, who learned his trade on that same backlot, you would have thought twice before coming into this town. Universal's rule then, as it appears to be today, was ride hard, punch first, and shoot fast, preferably from each hip.

The picture of Hollywood that has come down from the middle Twenties, when I started to work as an assistant director at Universal, is of a world of gay parties, swimming pools, and eccentric movie stars. It wasn't that way at Universal. Our big star was Laura La Plante. Under Carl Laemmle, the studio made a "bread and

99

butter" program of Westerns and comedies that garnered no fame but did make money. We worked hard. We had to. Uncle Carl expected it.

When I started work there, I still often daydreamed about Mary Hilton, wondering whether we might have had any kind of a life together. As for Rosika, my girl in the old country, time and space had caught up with my tender regard, I am afraid to say. She lived on in my memory as the most lovely, the most beautiful girl I had ever known, but I knew our youthful dream of a life together was an impossibility.

With Mary I held back from marriage, mainly, I must now confess, because I was young and ambitious enough to regard her family's wealth and position as an impossible handicap. Not so Mary. In letters that arrived almost every day she urged me to overlook the handicap of her millions and to recall the pledge of love she had offered.

But one day I got a letter from her. "I'm getting married," she wrote. "My family insists on it. I have no alternative unless you send for me."

Something told me it was better that way. I often wonder why I resisted Mary, for I loved her as a man loves in his twenties, on faith and hope mostly. Above all I think I would not marry her because I felt that it would take me away from making motion pictures. I got that much of a kick out of my job.

Imagine my surprise when a few weeks later I drove up to a little bungalow I had bought out in Malibu to find a man in a stiff-starched collar waiting for me. He knew my name, invited himself in, and came right to the point.

"Miss Hilton has been writing you. May we have her letters?"

"Who are you?"

He presented me with a crisp engraved card bearing the name of a famous law firm.

"Why should I give you those letters? They belong to me."

"Miss Hilton is getting married."

"So she's written me."

"I don't know if you know her family. They are most discreet. I can offer you ten thousand dollars."

"Ten thousand dollars!" I exclaimed. "For what?"

I can still say today that I had no idea why such an offer should be made to me. My innocence of mind only confused the attorney; the more I protested, the higher he bid for Mary's letters. He went to twenty-five thousand.

Finally I got the point. "It may come as a surprise to you," I said, "but if I loved Mary less *I'd* marry her. Maybe this is a mistake a man makes in his life. I wouldn't sell any memory of Mary under any circumstances. If she wants those letters back, you tell her to write me and they'll be in the mail that day."

The lawyer snapped shut his brief case. His eyes were dark, unshining. "Either you're a fool or you're very clever," he said.

Ten days later I got a note from Mary asking me to keep her letters if I liked. She enclosed a newspaper story about her forthcoming wedding. I remember it was chilly that night at the beach, even though it was September. I built a fire and burned all her letters without rereading any of them.

I worked harder than ever after that. My friends were simple people who liked to visit my little cottage at the beach while I put together a goulash like we used to make in Hungary.

There was some fun, though. There was the time when Willy Wyler brought a company to Big Bear to make a Western picture. It was discovered, once the crew and the players were ready to go to work on their remote mountain location, that though everything had been carefully prepared for, every last prop stowed or ready for shooting, someone had forgotten to bring along the scripts.

The oversight was so tremendous that Willy decided to go ahead anyway. "I read the script back at the studio," he said. "These Westerns are all alike anyway. I remember how this one went."

He recalled it brilliantly. The company was able to return to Universal City on schedule. But when the executives saw what Willy had got on film, they fired him promptly. He remembered the script all right, but he remembered one he had already shot for the studio. Luckily for the American film industry, the great director who was later to make *Dodsworth* and *Wuthering Heights* and *The Best Years of Our Lives* got his job back again. I'll wager the picture Willy shot from memory was better than what anyone with a shooting script beside him could have made.

Willy didn't care that he was fired. He was brilliant, fearless, and he didn't have much taste for work in those days anyway. I am always astonished how many great artists I have known and worked with feel that way. Lionel Barrymore once said his whole life had been a long campaign to avoid work. Then there was Wallace Beery. I met him when I was an assistant director at the Long Island studio. Wallie had a superb ability for getting the most pay for the least work. He was much like the man we got to know in a score of screen characterizations, gruff, lovable, and with just enough of the charming scamp in him to make him interesting. Nothing pleased him so much as being paid for not-working.

Gregory La Cava followed this line too, but he didn't care if he got paid or not, just so long as he didn't have to work. Greg has gone from the scene but in the middle Twenties it was obvious to anyone who had eyes in his head that this brilliant, spirited man was a true film genius. He had a wild, mad streak to him; he was unpredictable, but everything he did was unique and had a stamp of genius to it.

But it remained for an extra I met in those days to insist on having greatness thrust on him. I was an assistant director, the All-Powerful who gave the slips to the extras that meant work or idleness the next day. It came as a surprise to me, then, that I heard from a crowd of them the snapping of fingers and the brusque call, "Hey, you, there. Come 'ere, will you?" I was so taken aback by this treatment, since I was used to a certain amount of deference, that I went over to see the brash young man.

"This is no way to talk to the assistant director," I told him. "Not if you want to get ahead."

"Who wants to get ahead?"

There was something bright about him, on the button, special. His name was Jack Oakie. I like to remember him as he was that day because in a sense he was my first discovery.

"I hoped you'd be sore at me," Jack said, "so I could go to the beach and soak up the sun without wondering whether I'd have to work or not tomorrow."

"Come on with me," I said.

I took him in to see Wesley Ruggles. One thing led to another, and before long Jack was under personal contract to Ruggles. Maybe Jack, rich and retired now, might have preferred idling away the years on the beach at Santa Monica to making the big money. If so, I hope he forgives me for having made him work for so long.

One Friday, the prospect of being unemployed myself hit me. A studio executive, Jules Bernheim, saw me walking out the gate. "Hey," he said. "Mr. Laemmle wants to see you Monday. Bright and early."

"What's it about?" I asked, trying to cover up my fright.

"He'll tell you," Bernheim answered, and walked away.

Recalling how suddenly, how capriciously, I had been fired in New York, I spent a restless, sleepless week end. I tried to remember all the vouchers I had signed, some hastily, some carelessly. There was the florist in Sacramento who had sent me a wrist watch after I had placed a large order with him. Shouldn't I have returned the watch? Imagine risking my whole career for a miserable watch that didn't keep correct time anyway. What about that work we had needed done when we were on location and which I paid for out of my petty cash? Some bookkeeper had turned this up and I was through. I defended myself a thousand times, prepared little speeches in which I would tell Laemmle that what I did every assistant did, that he must have pity on me, that I would make good every penny the company thought I had short-changed it.

Bernheim was waiting for me that Monday. "Come on," he said darkly. "He's waiting for you."

"Can you tell me what it's about? What have I done?"

"You'll find out."

Laemmle looked up at me through thick rimless glasses. "Sit down," he snapped.

I sat. On the edge of a chair.

"You speak German?"

I looked over at Bernheim, standing near the door. Bernheim nodded. I didn't speak German, not well, but I had enough to get by on.

"I said, Do you speak German?"

"Yes."

"How'd you like to go to Europe?"

I was so surprised that I said, "What for?"

The old man shook his head testily, as though a fly had settled on his nose. He dug into a pile of papers on his desk. "I'll see you later," he snapped at me. The interview was over.

Outside, Bernheim was also annoyed with me. "What'd you want to say 'what for' for?" he demanded. "You confused him."

"But what did he ask me that for?"

Then Bernheim told me. Universal had a lot of blocked money in Europe and they were going to use some of it in making pictures abroad. They had already sent Paul Kohner there to head up the operation. But Kohner needed help and Bernheim had recommended me. And what had I done? I'd asked, "What for?"

A few days later Laemmle called me in again. He had made up his mind I was to go, without asking me, and about all that remained for him to decide was my salary. He pointed out that the American dollar went far in Europe and that my salary would reflect this.

I wasn't anxious to go for any long period of time. But the idea of returning home, to see my parents and my family, was irresistible. Laemmle assured me the whole assignment would take no longer than three months.

"One thing more," I told him. "I had a miserable trip here in the steerage. I want to go back like a king."

The old man, an immigrant himself years before from Laupheim, Germany, twinkled. He thought it a splendid idea.

"Your first picture's going to be a polo picture. You know anything about polo?"

"Oh, sure," I said carelessly. "Everything." That night I went to the library and took out every book that had any connection with polo.

In the weeks while I got ready for my European venture, *The Jazz Singer* burst noisily on the movie horizon. Sound pictures were still a doubtful quality. There were many who said the nature of the film medium called for silent action. The so-called "talkies" were a fad, they contended, and would soon lose their novelty. At Universal "sound effects" were being added to pictures that were already made. A revolution was taking place but I was no part of it. My only concern was mastering the game of polo. Looking back on it now, I cannot help shaking my head.

13. "Never Disturb Memories"

ONCE upon a time a handsome knight in shining armor encountered a beautiful princess on a meadow dotted with bright flowers. They had only to look briefly at each other to know that they loved truly. "Save me," the princess entreated the knight. "I am being brought to a black tower, there to be imprisoned because of reasons I cannot understand."

"I will rescue you," the handsome knight promised.

"I know you will," the princess said. "I will wait for you."

The knight made it his life's only purpose to save his beloved and make her his. The odds against him were always high. He was alone, in a strange country, always battling against forces greater than his, secure behind their fortress walls.

But he was undeterred. Every time he was repulsed in battle, he waited only for his wounds to heal, or his bones to mend, before he assailed the black tower again. His love for the beautiful princess was so great that no defeat could discourage him, no worldly pleasure entrap him.

For many years he stormed the tower without success,

without even a sight of his beloved. Then one day, executing a maneuver with brilliance and daring, he was able to breach the fortress. He raced to his beloved's side in the black tower, breaking down the door to rescue her.

He encountered a plain, pallid creature. "Where is your mistress, the princess?" he demanded breathlessly.

"I am the princess," the faded beauty replied.

"But you cannot be!" the knight insisted. "The princess was my true love. She was beautiful! She was exquisite. She was a creature like none who ever lived. I know because I saw her with these eyes, held her in these arms."

The princess turned to a table and picked up a hand mirror which she gave the knight. "And the knight I knew was a young man unmarked by the scars of battle, unbattered by the battle-axe. I remember him well too." She gave him the mirror. "Do you?"

After my return to Europe, my old teacher Schwarz told me this story one afternoon as we lay on a grassy knoll that overlooked the river that ran by our town. It is my belief that he made it up himself. It sounds like him, full of poetry, but with a bitter-sweet quality to it.

Schwarz asked me how it felt to come home again. I told him. He smiled and made up the little fairy tale. What I told him was everything that had to do with my homecoming. I was young enough to be shamelessly happy about returning home bearing all the signs and tokens of a successful man. My first thought—and I don't want to sound modest saying this—was that my parents were proud of me. Our family always had a very strong bond that kept us together. In my years in America I had brought over my brothers Johnny and Emil; I helped my sister

Lenka immigrate to the United States and another sister, Sari, to Canada. I often asked my father and mother to come here too. But my father believed he owed an obligation to his own mother and father to stay near them, especially since they were very old, and his own family obligation overrode any personal wish on his part.

We were a close-knit family. It was part of my heritage. In all the years I had been away, I wrote home at least once a week, with the exception of the months when I was stranded in Hamburg. I always sent a little something from my savings to my parents. No one told me to do so; I did it out of no sense of "obligation," or "duty," or because it was expected of me. It was natural. It was my pleasure. When I was making nine dollars a week, I sent home two. If I made thirty, I sent home seven. The more I could send, the better I felt. I wasn't doing it for them, perhaps; maybe I was doing it for myself.

So I was glad to come home. It was, in fact, one of the concessions that I exacted from Laemmle for going to Europe. I wanted four weeks at home before I took up my duties in Berlin. I was preceded by all the flurries and flourishes of which Universal's European publicity people were capable.

On the *Mauretania* I had the good luck to run into an Argentine polo team. I gave a cocktail party for them and used this priceless opportunity to get background for my first picture from a team of international champions. But outside of this, I gave little thought to anything but seeing my home town again, my family, and Rosika.

The town disappointed me. The river was dirty. It was narrow. I'd remembered it as a wide, clear stream. The bridge that I'd thought so adorable was shabby; I'd been thinking of it as painted white, with a picture-book quality to it. When I saw it, I could only think that the wood it was made of was ready to fall apart from rot. The synagogue needed a coat of paint; inside, the benches looked as though they could take some work too. The windows were dirty. The streets were muddy. The houses in the town, the people who stood on the street to greet me, the hometown boy who had gone to America and proved true what they'd all been told about the place, all filled me with sadness and pity.

My family had changed. Only my sister Helen was at home, the one child my father was keeping beside him. He had "lost" the others, whom I had helped to come to America, but Helen was still his. She had become the-daughter-who-stays-home. My mother had not been entirely well while I was gone; they had kept this from me in their letters. In their eyes, I suppose I had changed too; I am sure of it; but they insisted I was the same person who had left eight years before.

I went out to the gypsy camp. The fiddlers were out of tune; they had no richness, no body. And where were all the pretty gypsy girls I remembered? They had all gone, or gotten old and fat.

And Rosika? I was told she had married some years before. At least I had not entirely forgotten the promise we made. I wanted to see her anyway.

I went to her house. She was very plain and, like the gypsy girls, had grown very fat. I told her about America. I said I liked it there. She said it must be very interesting. I said it was. She said she would like to go there some day.

She introduced me to her children. I patted them on the head, looked at my watch, and said I thought that it was time to be going. Was I going to be here long? she asked. I said I would spend some weeks with my parents. That was very nice, she said.

These are the things I told Schwarz on the river bank before he told me his little fairy tale.

"What about me?" he said. "You're not going to say I've changed. I still am harassed by too many pupils, too many duties, and too little pay. I still drink, if anything, a little more than ever." His eyes twinkled. "Especially now that I do not have a student who waters my schnapps."

"No, you haven't changed. I wonder why that is?"

"Probably because you had no illusions about me. The dream changes, the reality remains." He took a drink and lay back, looking up at the sky just as he had done so many years before. "If you can forgive a sinful old teacher a bit of moralizing, I'll give you a little rule. Never disturb memories. Nothing is so beautiful as a memory."

After that, whenever I came home to visit my parents (and I came as often as my duties for Universal permitted), I only went to see them. I had no illusions about the town. Sometimes I berated myself for this attitude. I said to myself that I must have grown worldly and cynical and could no longer appreciate the simple things of life. But I have applied Schwarz's rule in other places and have found it to be very true. To this day I wish I could think of the town I was born in and grew up in as I remembered it, and not as I saw it when I returned.

14. The Berlin Years

As late as the end of 1930 there were only four efficient sound studios in all of Germany. And yet, if I expected to find a makeshift movie operation in Germany, I was soon disabused. Among other priceless heritages the German people threw away with both hands after 1933 we may count their film industry. Soon after my arrival in Berlin, I came to the conclusion, which I have never had reason to change, that the German film was in a fair way to capture the world audience.

The German film makers were slow to take up sound, but once they accepted it, they learned all there was to learn from the real innovators and masters. They struggled along with too few sound stages and other handicaps. On the other hand, their technicians, their cameramen and directors were among the most creative and imaginative in the world. Today our own film industry, as does our science, medicine, and art, in a sense owes a debt to Hitler for enriching us with their talent when he made life impossible for them in the Third Reich.

The German film industry was headed in the last years before Hitler by a group of independent producers. These were mostly promoters, men who could raise the backing, or upon whom the creative talent could lay all the workaday problems of making pictures. The producer was expected to have no hand in anything that involved script or shooting, or even casting, except, of course, to raise the money to see that everything was done to the director's satisfaction.

There was but one exception to this rule. This was the great organization known as UFA, which stood for Universum Film A.G. Headed by Eric Pommer, UFA had a huge and efficient studio just outside of Berlin at Neubabelsberg.

The history of the German film industry is worth going into here to provide the background for my stay in the country where I remained, not for the three months Carl Laemmle had promised me, but until, sickened by the Nazi seizure of power, I left for Budapest in 1933.

After the First World War the German silent films won artistic laurels all over the world. Murnau, Pabst, Lubitsch, Dupont gave the camera scope, vision and movement such as the American film had not yet been able to achieve. I am not at one with the highbrow critics in liking what the German film makers *said* in their pictures. But the talent and the genius that went into their morbid, twisted stories cannot be denied.

At the end of the Twenties, Pommer visited Hollywood to learn what he could about Hollywood's popular touch. He returned about the same time that I was sent to work with Paul Kohner.

The impact of sound among the German film people was not as instantaneous as it must have been (I was not there) in America. Mostly they were content to sit back, adopting a wait-and-see attitude. Also, in Germany you had many more of the film intellectuals who were simply and unqualifiedly opposed to sound. They believed that the film was a "visual" medium and they contended that the addition of a sound track only detracted from the film's purpose. Like most film intellectuals, they took a very dim view of the audience and wanted to go their own way, even if the audience would not go with them.

The opening of *The Jazz Singer* in Berlin was an immediate sensation. The crowds lined up before the theatre showed there was no question that sound had a vast popular appeal. As has so often happened, the public was far ahead of the artists. Audiences accepted sound; they were willing to overlook the technical deficiencies which troubled us. When the sound went out of "sync"—the dialogue and music were on an accompanying platter like a victrola record instead of running on an accompanying track, as today—the people merely overlooked it.

In January 1929 the Germans made their first feature film in sound. It was called *I Kiss Your Hand, Madame.* The song it featured was not long in crossing the Atlantic to become as popular in America as it was in Europe. *I Kiss Your Hand, Madame* starred the singer Harry Liedtke and a Berlin night club artist named Marlene Dietrich. The picture itself was a misbegotten creature. Most of the time it was nothing more than a silent film, but every now and then a few feet of sound photography was inserted. Harry Liedtke sang the famous tune.

The picture was a huge success, proving once again

114

that only the technicians and critics eat their hearts out about technical failings. The picture established Marlene Dietrich as a great personality in Germany. Pommer sent to Hollywood for the director Josef Von Sternberg, who had brilliantly directed Emil Jannings in *The Last Command* and had made a violent story of gangsters and killings, *Underworld*. Sternberg was a former cameraman, a specialist in moody shots, visual symbolism, and many such things which appealed to the Germans.

The picture Sternberg was to do was *The Blue Angel*, with Dietrich and Emil Jannings. The story was by Heinrich Mann and it was one of those things in which a hitherto contented bourgeois Herr Professor falls for a bad girl and thereby ruins what was once a good life.

The Blue Angel was important for bringing to the world the beauty and talent of Marlene Dietrich, whom I shall talk about in a more personal way later; it is also important because it showed that the Germans were quick to learn how to use sound creatively.

In America the popular pictures then were mostly "musicals," tepid little stories in which the music was "cued" in with all the grace of a locomotive backing into a roundhouse. "Isn't it a beautiful night?" the heroine would ask the hero. "Yes," he would murmur into her bashful ear, "the stars are out tonight." And he would sit down at a piano and start to play and sing a song called "The Stars Are Out Tonight."

The German film workers were much impressed by René Clair's *Sous les Toits de Paris*. This masterpiece was the first film to integrate sound and sight in a light musi-

115

cal, to show that the sound track was not necessarily the enemy of the lens.

In a matter of months great German musicals began to come out of the Berlin studios. In 1930 there was *Two Hearts in Three-Quarter Time,* and *Congress Dances.* They were soon followed by *I and the Empress, Victor and Victoria,* and Pabst's freehand version of John Gay's *The Beggar's Opera, The Three-Penny Opera,* with a score by Kurt Weill.

While Americans were still using creaky devices in our musicals, in *Congress Dances* the Germans were doing things that to my startled eyes were revolutionary. In one scene, for example, Lilian Harvey is driving through the country in an open carriage. She is singing and as she passes people of various kinds, they take up the song she sings in her carriage.

Years later, when I returned to Hollywood, I was still encountering hard-headed realists who assured me that this kind of thing simply would not work. Where was the orchestra that was accompanying the singer? they asked me. And how did the people she passed know what key to sing in, what the words of the song were, and so on? The Germans, under René Clair's tutelage, showed that people believed because what they had to believe was worth believing.

In any event, when I started to work in Berlin, I found a film industry that, as I say, was capable of capturing the world market. The Germans were expanding, not only their physical movie-making plants, but their point of view. They welcomed talent; they were good to it. They were telling tales that had some appeal to vast audiences.

To keep up with them, I had to learn what they had learned. And I had to learn fast.

When I was ready to go to work, Paul Kohner greeted me affably. "You know what your first picture's going to be?" he asked me.

"Sure. The polo picture."

"Right. Come on, let's go and meet your star."

We went into an adjoining room where sat a medium-height man, rather darkly complexioned. "Joe Pasternak," Paul said, "this is Eddie Polo."

It was months before I knew Kohner well enough to reveal my embarrassment. The fact is that I had never even heard of Eddie Polo, who had been a great silent star, hero of athletic serials and such. He had gone into retirement about the time I arrived in America and it was Laemmle's idea to bring him back in Europe where he had some kind of following.

I had been an assistant director. Now I was a producer. It was not always an easy transition, for where before I executed someone else's orders, now I was giving the orders. I also had my own authority and I had to learn just how to use it, and when, and if.

The director of the Polo picture was Ernest Laemmle, a nephew of my boss's back in Hollywood. The nephew cannot be said to have been all that a new producer would look for in a director. When he did not arrive late, he did not turn up for work at all. This latter situation is the worst torture that can be inflicted on any producer of motion pictures. And no one can exactly fire the big boss's nephew.

Or he doesn't want to, if he can possibly help it. Certainly not on his first picture.

I compromised by docking young Mr. Laemmle's pay for his tardiness and his absences. And when he did not show up, I did not let it stop our shooting. I simply took over the director's chair myself. By the end of the picture I was having no trouble with young Laemmle whatsoever.

Berlin in those years was the most fabulous, the most sinful, most gay, colorful, and saddest city in the world.

Everybody spoke of it as a dying city and yet its vitality was endless. Perhaps vitality is not the right word. It was restless, feverish, wild. If you walked down the Kurfuerstendam, every few yards you were accosted and solicited by creatures of every description: elegantly turned-out ladies with the grace, breeding, and *hauteur* of the aristocracy; androgynes; men in women's clothes; women in men's clothes; street walkers in high boots.

And beneath it all was hunger and unrest. We have the benefit of hindsight today, but even then one could see that such a world must be headed for an explosion. Hitler? He was a joke. A few sub-moronic people, the *Lumpenproletariat,* would fall for his nonsense. In Prussia, where Berlin is located, his party had little popular following.

I had many friends who insisted that the stories we must make should reflect this troubled, disordered world. I rejected this idea for two reasons: first, it is my opinion that the movies cannot compete with newspaper headlines. Our stories cannot be as immediate, as intense, even as full of surprises. If in a story you had, say, two mortal enemies like Hitler and Stalin suddenly embracing each

118

other as they did in 1939, your audience would hoot in derision. Not only that, but I was a foreigner in Germany and I did not regard it as my business (even if I had a taste for it) to make morbid documentary-toned films about the sad state of postwar Germany.

And then it was not my natural inclination, as I have remarked before. In Berlin I formed whatever philosophy of making pictures I have. The world was sad, disordered, insane. Some people thought it their duty (these people always speak of conscience and integrity and so on) to tell their stories about this world. That is their right. I was as troubled as they, but I thought, and still think, I can help more by making people laugh, by giving them a moment of lightness and delight, of sweetness and charm, in a world that has always been wrong.

No doubt the world is full of stinkers and misery and ugliness and hatred. I decided my pictures would show clean-looking people; they would be full of fun, filled with the joy of life, fun, lovemaking, singing and dancing.

When Kohner left we were on the very best of terms. He was anxious to return to America and was able to persuade the high command at Universal that I would not let their European operation go to pieces.

One of the first things I learned in Berlin is that a movie maker is only as good as the talent he surrounds himself with. The central one, the heart of the film matter, is the writer. A good director can do wonders with an inadequate script; but no one can make a good picture out of a bad script, any more than we can make that silk purse out of a sow's ear.

It was natural for me to base my operation on writers.

Thus I met a young man, tall, delicate-nosed, and wearing, as he does today, spectacles. His experience was limited, but Henry Koster impressed me at once as a real talent. He had the quality of enthusiasm, as well as an ability to blend character and plot in the telling of his stories. He worked for me frequently and when I saw that his real interest lay in directing, I gave him a chance to direct. I am taking no bows, for Bobby Koster's talent would have been discovered by somebody else, if not by me. His genius is his own and he need be grateful to no one for it. But I'm glad to have been there at the beginning of the career of the director of *The Robe,* not to mention the first Deanna Durbin pictures which we made together in Hollywood.

Another young writer who impressed me was Billy Wilder. I believe that at the time I met him, Billy had had a success with a story of his called *One Sunday Afternoon.* He had had a success, but he needed a job. I liked him at once. He was, well—he was Billy Wilder, brilliant, keen and corrosive. Also, every story he ever did bore the stamp of his own personality. That he was able to do this on assignments for me was remarkable, especially when the titles of some of our minor epics in which he figured are recalled. *A Tango for You* ought to give you an idea. And yet if Billy worked on the script, it could only have been written by him.

And then there was Felix Jackson, who is now ably producing *Studio One* on television. Felix had a knack for charming tales about nice people; he could make them believable without being drivelish about it. In and out of marriage, he was invaluable and he did not let the collecting of wives interfere with his work. Besides, his wives, past and present, were without exception charming, beautiful, gracious, and only a damned fool could have resisted marrying any one of them; and Felix is no fool.

In Berlin, too, I met two friends who have been close to me ever since. Nicky Brodszky was a young, handsome, and extremely gifted pianist-composer with a couple of minor operettas to his credit. I wanted to commission him to write the score for a picture, but he was a Hungarian and we were handcuffed by German labor restrictions.

Years later I ran into Nicky again in Budapest, where he had returned when Hitler took over in Germany. He was playing the piano in 1933 in the Café New York, a little cellar club in the heart of the city, unique because it was the only establishment in town without gypsy music. He wrote several scores for my pictures, but you couldn't keep Nicky away from a piano. He seemed to float over the keyboard, inventing melodies, playing American popular tunes, his bench circled with the most lovely girls in town. Years later, after the phenomenal success of "Be My Love" in one of my American pictures, he told me he thought it was a little tune he used to play in the Café New York. I wouldn't be surprised. His music was always marvelous.

I had always wanted to meet Szoke Szakall, whom we knew in this country as S. Z. ("Cuddles") Sakall. It will be recalled that he was the first comedian I had ever seen on a stage. In Berlin he was a great and popular figure, on the stage, in films; he wrote his own material; wrote stories and sketches for the humorous weeklies; he was famous as a great offhand wit. (An offhand wit is someone who isn't always trying to show you how funny he is.)

The problem was how to meet Szakall. One evening, blue, bored, and quailing before the prospect of another dinner of robust German cooking, complete with *kartoffelkloesse*, *kartoffel*-this and *kartoffel*-that, I remember that I'd heard the Szakalls, who reputedly set the finest Hungarian table in the German capital, were having a dinner party.

I rang their doorbell, batted my baby-blues with all the innocence I could muster, and said: "My secretary accepted for me. I'm Joe Pasternak."

Szakall himself came to the door, standing beside his butler in some confusion. "You're not Joe Pasternak," he insisted. "Pasternak is a big American. You're a short Hungarian."

When they believed me, the Szakalls proved gracious and their cook's ability hadn't been overrated a bit. Bozsi and Jani Szakall became my especially dear friends. Jani worked for me in pictures abroad and later in this country. He was one of the most amusing, witty men I've ever encountered and when he passed away the world not only lost one of its most charming players but I lost a priceless friend.

Later, I was doing an historical epic out at the UFA Studio at Neubabelsberg. It starred and was directed by William Dieterle. I don't remember how I got involved with it; the dialogue was very formal and flowery and all the men wore beards. This by itself should have forewarned me.

I dropped by the set one day and found almost half

the crew gone. "Where's everybody?" I asked the assistant director.

"They're over on the next stage."

"What's on the next stage?"

"Haven't you been there yet?" He looked at me as though I was a man from another world. "You've never seen such legs." It was obvious he was far more intrigued with what was happening there than he was with King Ludwig II, the hero of my epic.

I wasted no time going to the next stage. Joe Sternberg was there doing the "Falling in Love Again" number from *The Blue Angel* with this Marlene Dietrich who was beginning to be so much talked about. Beginning, I say. When I saw how Joe was handling the number and got a look at those lovely legs, I could see that what was attracting my crew would soon be doing the same for cash-paying customers.

What magnetism! How she moved! And that voice: I was convinced she could be seductive merely asking the time of day. I kept in the background, planning my next move. I wanted to meet her, but the problem was how? Joe Sternberg was keeping her under lock and key on the set. It took me some days to figure out just what to do. Long enough so that even Dieterle observed that I was spending more time on Sternberg's stage than on his. Dieterle complained bitterly. "Aren't you interested in your own picture?" he berated me.

"Of course, Bill. Sure. I'll be there right away."

Finally it occurred to me that here I was, a Universal Pictures executive. Oughtn't I to begin negotiations, to investigate whether the possessor of those beautiful legs would be interested in a Hollywood contract? I broached the subject to Sternberg and asked him if I might send Marlene my card and visit with her between shots. He said it would be all right.

In a few moments her maid came up to me. "The *gnädige Fräulein* will see you now."

It was a blistering hot day, I remember. I had been carrying my coat over my arm, so I put it on again, followed the maid and waited discreetly at the door.

"Come in," a silken voice beckoned.

I walked in. Marlene, wreathed coolly in a sheer peignoir and nothing else, shimmering like the moon on a cloudy night, outstretched a long bare arm. I felt the thermometer rise. I tugged at my collar. "Hot, isn't it?" I offered.

"Do you think so?"

In her gossamer chiffon she may have wondered why I kept mopping my brow, but if so she gave me no sign.

She said she would be quite willing to entertain an offer from Universal. I said I would wire them.

That was my first meeting with Marlene. I met her once or twice after that before she went to America. Later I made a number of pictures with her. But I have often thought of our first meeting, for it was, as I think of it. pure Dietrich: daring, unforgettable, touched with her unique personal magic.

Universal owned two huge movie houses in Berlin. They were managed by a man named Flader, a German who had gone to America, become a citizen, and had been sent back by the company.

Shortly after I arrived in Berlin, he had me over to dinner. I regarded it as one of those matters of protocol which would call for a return dinner on my part until the formalities between us could be done with once and for all and we could each go our separate ways.

Flader had two lovely daughters. One of them, Margaret, became my secretary. Some time later we were married. An autobiographer, I realize, has a duty not to dissemble, nor to hold back on matters which are climactic in his life. I have tried to recall how it was in those days and how I felt, but the details elude me. Psychologize me no psychologists: the significance of this is quite clear to me.

It leads me to a somewhat belated estimate of myself at the time. I was busy but I was lonely. Events, problems, people crowded in on me at every moment but a deep sense of apartness assailed me. This is not the way a man should marry. I understand that. But my obligation to you is to record the truth as it happened, not as I should have liked it to have happened.

Therefore I must also tell you that from the very first I must have failed Margaret in many ways. Our marriage was under a cloud from the very beginning. It was my fault and there it is, whether I like it or not.

The immediate effect, however, was to cause me to throw myself into my work and the people involved in it, deeper than ever. This did the marriage no good. And as the relationship between Margaret and me paled, it caused me to work even harder. It was an insanely vicious cycle.

* * *

Kohner and I had cabled Universal City for permission to sign Marlene. I said she would be a great international star and she was willing to go to Hollywood.

I was turned down.

Foreigners, they said. All these Europeans, cozying up to each other.

This was my usual experience. Kohner and I had seen a preview of *Mädchen in Uniform*. It wasn't my cup of tea but it turned out to be a huge success in Germany. It didn't take much acumen to figure out that it ought to do fairly well in the United States. We took an option to buy the film for fifteen thousand dollars.

Universal City said no. Who'd want to see an arty European thing? Those foreigners again!

Two Hearts in Three-Quarter Time was another instance. Again, "No!" Finally it seeped into my thick skull that any suggestion from Europe was written off as soon as it arrived.

After Marlene was turned down, I began to realize that in Europe I was an island, apart from the studio's real operation. The only notice they took of my pictures was when the New York critics caught them in one of the art-houses and gave them a good notice.

Also it came to me that in Hollywood they were forgetting that I was an American.

Twice a year I used to visit my parents. I had bought them a somewhat more comfortable house. My father still functioned as *shammas,* devoted as always to his religious duties and faith, and happy. My mother was not well, but at least she was now able to secure good care.

In Budapest, on the way back to Berlin, I happened to see a play starring Franciska Gaal. She was one of Hungary's leading actresses but this was the first time I had seen her. I was enchanted. Franciska had a childlike quality underlined with a woman's knowing heart. She was in her twenties, but appeared to be even younger. I went to see her and told her I wanted to bring her to Berlin and star her in a picture.

"But I don't know a word of German," she assured me.

"No matter," I said. "If I prepare a script will you come and do it?"

"Of course. But I don't think you will when you consider that I might as well be speaking Chinese."

In trying to describe Franciska Gaal's talent, one can only compare her with, say, Gertrude Lawrence or Mary Martin. She was perfect in whatever she did, song, dance, comedy, drama. I was determined to use her in a picture in spite of the language barrier.

A few months later I brought her the script and the score by Franz Waxman for a film to be called *Paprika*. I had to read it to her, translating it into Hungarian as I went along.

"I never thought you'd be foolish enough to go through with this," Franciska said. "As long as you have, I'll keep my end of the bargain."

Paprika became one of the greatest successes of the postwar period in Europe. Franciska played her part by learning her speeches phonetically. She never knew quite what she was saying but she became the big star of German pictures just the same, as she well deserved to be.

I made a number of pictures with Franciska Gaal, each

as successful as the last. Everybody loved them. I heard that even Hitler, whom no one considered a joke any longer, adored her. He insisted that someone so pretty and so charming could not be Jewish. There must be a genealogical mistake somewhere, he said.

It was about then that I began to make my pictures as I've made them ever since.

One way is to buy the established hit, the smash Broadway play, the Book-of-the-Month, get Cole Porter or Irving Berlin to write the score, Tennessee Williams to write the script, cast it with the mostest of the bestest, and you have a picture.

Not my way. Not interesting.

Safer perhaps, but no fun.

The way I learned to do it was to begin with a little creative spark, mine, someone else's, all of ours. You make it all yours, collectively. The story, the players, the score. It was your idea. Not another *South Pacific* brought to the films, but your little baby, your own, though it may emerge a scrawny thing and though the august confraternity of critics may kick it from here to breakfast for the sake of turning a funny line.

Universal's executives were still pursuing a narrow, chauvinistic policy. They refused to be impressed by Franciska Gaal's success or even by the grosses of the pictures in which she starred.

Many of the pictures we made in Europe were later done in English in this country, usually by producers who bought them from Universal. When Buddy De Sylva left that studio, for example, one of the conditions of his settling his contract was that they give him the rights to

Little Mother, which was one of our German pictures with a score by Nicholas Brodszky. In its American version it was known as *Bachelor Mother* and was as big a success with Ginger Rogers as it had been with Franciska Gaal. *Top Hat*—with Fred Astaire and Ginger Rogers—was another re-do of one of our German films.

This was annoying, but other, larger considerations were beginning to force themselves into the lives of all of us.

15. *Farewell to Berlin*

ONE of my recurrent daydreams takes me back to a time I was traveling across Germany and went to the dining car for dinner.

There, sitting at a table across the aisle from me, were four men: Adolf Hitler, Hermann Goering, Paul-Joseph Goebbels, and Ernst Roehm.

If I had known then what I know now, how much agony and pain I might have spared the world with a well-placed grenade or a machine gun! I know it is murder even as I daydream, but the loathing is so deep within me that I am even prepared to do murder.

In a way, though I did not know it that day in the railroad car, my life was to be touched by those of the Nazi leaders at many points.

Two years after my arrival in Berlin, Universal sent over to Germany for release the prints of Lewis Milestone's great antiwar film *All Quiet on the Western Front*.

Hitler's National-Socialist Party, which had started in Bavaria and Thuringia, had never been able to gain much strength in the state of Prussia, which continuously had a government that was largely democratic. Then Hitler ordered Goebbels to Berlin to head up the Party organization. Goebbels knew he needed an issue to find out just how far the Berlin police would go in combating the Nazi Party and also to create a situation in which the dark, violent tradition in German life which the Weimar Republic tried so feebly to arrest could erupt into fascism.

Goebbels found his target in *All Quiet*. The selection was not capriciously or hastily made. It was a picture that dealt with German soldiers, made by foreigners, Jews at that. It showed that Germany had lost the war when everybody knew it would have won but for the stab in the back.

All Quiet opened in Berlin in December of 1930. It was a great popular success instantly. It struck a responsive chord in the German people, for it was their story truly and magnificently told. But the Nazis demonstrated in the streets of the West End against the picture and carried on violently in front of the theatre. The ultra-nationalist press, though not Nazi, editorialized against the picture. The Nazis used this support for larger demonstrations.

The Berlin police moved against them gently, timidly. The Nazis increased the violence of their demonstrations and when the police refused to be provoked, Goebbels took this as a sign of official cowardice and knew now that whatever he chose to do, whether against this film or in other cases, he need not worry about counter-action.

A few days after the premiere *All Quiet* was ordered withdrawn from circulation by the Chief Censor. Only in June 1931 was limited permission given for showing the film before specialized audiences—trade unions, study groups, and the like. Later that summer, after certain cuts were made in the film, it was allowed once more to be shown in public. Goebbels had moved on to other fields by that time.

Meanwhile, to my astonishment and dismay, the Nazis continued to gain more popular support. I had an office sub-manager, the "little man" the Germans always talked about. I listened sympathetically to his problems, and they were many. I arranged for him to get small raises wherever I could as his family and his problems increased. "Don't worry," he told me, "the German people will never go Nazi. This is just a mood."

But even German films were reflecting the huge sentimental attachment for the nationalistic past. An epic of the German undersea submarine campaign was being shot at one of the studios. It was called *Morgenrot,* or *Dawn.* I was anxious to see how strong an antiwar spirit would run through the picture.

It was to be premiered on January 30, 1933. But a government fell and the senile Hindenburg asked Hitler, despite his lack of a popular majority at the last election, to form a government. The evening after taking office, Hitler and his friends attended a gala, delayed premiere of *Dawn* at the UFA Palace. Everybody was there, even all the "nice" Nationalists who had always assured you they wanted a place in the sun but deplored Hitler's violence, and the above-politics monarchists, including the Crown Prince.

The picture pleased the premiere audience completely. Its title is symbolic, for it presaged a new day in German film making. The picture glorified the German U-boats and the sink-without-mercy policy they had pursued throughout the war. There was not a peaceful, compassionate note in the whole length of it.

The next morning, reading how the picture had been well received by its notable audience, I looked up at the calendar and wondered how long I could stay on.

My answer was not long coming. One evening at dinner the radio gave word that the Reichstag had been set afire. The Nazis immediately used this as a pretext to institute a campaign of reprisal against all their opponents, without exception. Next day began that black campaign of economic boycott against the Jewish stores, or, I should say, so-called Jewish stores, for most of them were owned by many shareholders.

I returned to my office. To my astonishment who should walk in but my meek sub-manager in full Nazi regalia. "All right," he said sharply. "From now on we take over. You ask permission of me for everything, understand?"

I told Henry Koster and a few others that I was getting out. I had not been molested. An American, I was safe. I know many innocent Americans went to Germany while the Nazis were in power and they came back and solemnly gave witness that there was no violence. But I know. I saw it. I saw the "little man" turn up in his Nazi uniform full of arrogance and hate, and full of contempt for us because he took kindness as a sign of weakness and stupidity. I saw the bullies in the streets, standing over ancient, gentle men, kicking them when they did not scrub the gutters to their satisfaction. My gorge was not iron enough to have stayed, despite my American passport.

16. The Pearl of the Danube

I MOVED our film-making operation to Budapest for a simple and, I must confess, selfish reason. I loved Budapest.

The prosy, workaday problems in the transfer were readily solved. The Hungarian government built a studio for us. We could make bilingual pictures with German-speaking actors from Vienna and Germany just as easily in Budapest as we could in Berlin. So it was not difficult for me to decide to move there. But I think I'd have gone to Budapest if I'd had to make our pictures in a damp wine cellar with Gujerati-speaking actors. I loved Budapest. I said that before, didn't I? As with a girl you are truly enamored of, you can't say the words often enough.

I loved Budapest. To me it always had a special magic, a poetry like no city in all the world. It was gay, but not neurotic and disordered, as was Berlin. It was small enough so that you felt the place was yours; yet it had the quality that distinguishes a city from a town: an endless variety of people and moods. The girls were beautiful and chic, which helps any city, and the men were good companions, which is almost as pleasant.

And they were all Hungarians.

To appreciate the Hungarian you have to like people with a touch of color and madness; you have to value charm for its own sake; and, most of all, you must accept the point of view that the best things in life are graciousness, good food, wine, music, and lovemaking. Work is an abomination, a curse on earth, a necessary evil, the unfortunate *condition humaine*. That man is successful who avoids it most rigorously; he who can manage gracefully without being smudged by labor is the most enviable in the whole world. A man is happy if he can achieve the good things of life with a minimum of effort. No one acquires money for its own sake, for the biggest fortune in the world doesn't begin to compare to a good dinner, wine, gypsy music, and a beautiful girl in candlelight. The only mercenary Hungarian I ever met was Ferenc Molnar. Curious how this most Hungarian of playwrights, this *minnesinger* of the charm and grace of Budapest life, should have been a penny-watcher with his eye more steadily fixed on the state of his investments than on a lovely ankle.

I recall once he and I were having tea in the Bristol lobby. A breathlessly pretty young thing, all crisp and shining, glowing with eagerness, rushed to our table. "You're Mr. Molnar, aren't you?" she said.

"I am," he said.

"Oh, Mr. Molnar, you must help me. I've read your plays. I love them. They're so often about how someone like me who has no money wins the heart of a rich man. How can I do this in life as you do it on the stage? How

136

can I get such a man to fall in love with me? Tell me, please, help me."

Molnar's face was a mask; not a muscle flickered. The girl's eyes sparkled like handfuls of emeralds; her mouth was parted slightly, waiting for a single word from the great playwright. Then Molnar said, coolly: "So you wish to meet a rich man?"

"Yes."

"And will you fall in love with him?"

"What use would his money be without love?"

"Tell me," he said quickly, his voice edged with an unmistakable sadness, "I am the rich man you want to meet, isn't that so?"

For a moment the girl could say nothing. Her head fell slightly. "Yes," she admitted.

"And this is all a trick to meet me, to talk to me?"

She nodded hopelessly. "I have fallen in love with you. I adore your plays. I adore the spirit behind them. The wit. I know you're successful—that doesn't make you less attractive. You live in a world beyond mine—yet I love you. That's why I've had to do this to meet you. I've been waiting for this moment."

"My dear girl," Molnar said, "you have been wasting your time." He turned his back to her, not even willing to throw away a witticism he might use in a play in dismissing the poor girl.

Needless to say, he later let me pick up the check. He always did. Poor chap, he was one of those mortals who despite their wealth remain convinced all their lives that they will die in the poorhouse.

Life among my friends in Budapest began just as the

sun was going down. The daily enemy, it must be remembered, was the sun. It was no "rosy-fingered dawn" for them; it did not "tip yon horizon." The sun meant the harsh yellow light of reality; it meant work, jobs, clerks, bill-collectors and landladies and tailors asking for a little something on account.

My friends arose for the new day about five. That would be p.m., of course not a.m. After a leisurely bath, they ate the meal that was called not *breakfast* but *first-meal*. If they were actors—and they often were—they'd go to the theatre until eleven or so. If not, they might work at their writing or music-making or rehearsing until that hour. The dinner hour was somewhere about midnight. There was no such thing as a "dinner date." The closest you might come to it would be if you said something to a friend like, "I may be at the Royale tonight, or the Hungaria." You arrived alone, saw a friend or two and sat with them. Others arrived; they joined the party. The American style of eating solo or with one friend would have been considered barbarous.

As for the girls, they were on their own too. Most of my friends had no telephones, regarding them as vile instruments whose only purpose was to permit certain loathsome characters to dun them more frequently. The only time a man actually made a firm date with a girl for a *diner à deux* was when they had just met and were in the fine, full flush of captivation. This was good for the first three or four meetings, but since my friends were always falling madly in love, small dinners happened more often than you might imagine.

After dinner everybody repaired to one of the many

138

gypsy cafés that bordered the Danube over on the Buda side of town. This might be at two or three in the morning. They might stay until four, taking a light supper, of course, later to head to a place back in town call the Kis Royale, which can only be described as an even noisier Lindy's with gypsy music.

Once the musicians, discouraged by the clamor of dishes and talk, so loud that they could not hear themselves, quit in disgust. A hush descended on the establishment. All talk, all activity ceased. Without the fiddles and cymbaloms in the background, life could no more go on than if someone had shut off the electricity. The customers and the management pleaded. The musicians played again, the incessant noices started once more, and everyone was happy—except the musicians, of course.

My friends did not know how to accept me. I made pictures as we did in America. Nicky Brodszky and the others contended that my "American" methods would never work. In France and Italy, I was informed, shooting schedules were pleasantly relaxed. I insisted that we begin work every morning at nine and wind up at six. Without exceptions. Hangovers, passionate romances, a surfeit of paprikash—these were no excuses.

The result was the sleepiest contingent of actors, writers, lyricists, and composers in all Europe. Naturally they could not break with long-established custom. You got home at dawn, you bathed, put on fresh clothes, cursed Pasternak and went to work when all the sensible people of the world were going to bed.

My people caught up with their sleep as best they could. The actors snoozed among the tangle of cables in the dark corners of the stages; I once observed an actress dead to the world, standing bolt upright in a tight-bodiced Maria Theresa gown. The writers and composers and lyricists were luckier, for if I came into their quarters and found them sleeping, they mumbled something about working on a great idea and would I close the door quietly, please?

I loved the night life. I took whatever I could of it, consonant with my duties as a production executive and a constitution with a deplorable tendency to wheeze, huff, and groan on anything less than six hours of repose. I envied those of my *confrères* who seemed able to manage on little or no sleep. If I hadn't seen that it could be done, I would doubt one could manage without regular sleep. Credit this to Budapest, say I.

It was in Budapest, too, that I began to make pictures much as I do now. The single element which I sought to instill in every venture was a sense of joyful, equal collaboration. I wanted no one to feel slighted, or to feel that his contribution was more, or less, significant than the next man's. This sometimes involved a use of the diplomat's art. One of my leading men, for example, drew me aside one afternoon to complain bitterly that Jani Szakall was getting all the laughs and would steal the picture. If I didn't speak to Jani about stopping his nonsense, the leading man would walk off the picture. I went to Jani and told him what our matinee idol had said. "All right," said he, "you tell him I'll give him the laughs if he gives me the girl."

When I think of those days I recall the fun, the laughter, and the marvelous Hungarians who pursued me relentlessly. The Hungarians are the greatest borrowers in the world and I imagine Polonius' advice to Laertes about "neither a borrower nor a lender be" must sound like the most foolish gibberish in translation. Everyone I knew borrowed and lent. It was understood, accepted, and thought nothing of. You went to dinner flush or broke and if in extreme circumstances you couldn't avoid the check or borrow enough to pay for it, you signed. It was understood that those with money always paid and those who were broke cadged. The theory was that when the cadgers had it, they would pick up the check. The only thing wrong with the theory was that the borrowers never seemed to have money.

Borrowing was not only an art, it was a business. I have already told of my chauffeur, Elemer, who furnished advance information on my moods and receptivity for a flat ten per cent of all sums borrowed. He was a small private entrepreneur. But there was an outfit in town that kept a file on how to make a big touch on your subject. *They* got twenty per cent. But their intelligence was impeccable. They could tell you that So-and-So found an appeal about ailing mothers irresistible. You must talk to him about the kind old lady who'd worked scrubbing floors so you could write, or paint, or compose, and how heartbroken she'd be if you failed, not to say starved. The next man, however, might be hard-hearted, but he was a cinch if you hit him without mercy. You stirred up a goulash of guilt feelings in him mercilessly and he came across.

Once I complained that every broke actor, writer, and director who needed money always came to see me.

"What do you expect?" Nicky Brodszky challenged me.

"Where else would they go? Who's making your kind of money?"

One of my friends, an actor, out of work, of course, asked me if I'd mind if he used my charge account to send a couple of toys to a nephew who was having a birthday.

"Of course," I said, "please do." I figured how much could a couple of toys for a child run me—ten dollars?

When I got the statement I saw that he had used it to the extent of one hundred and sixty good American dollars.

"For a toy or two!" I exploded. "That's outrageous! How can you spend that kind of money?"

He put up his hand to stop this unseemly display of temper and unreasonableness. "Joe," he reminded me, "what difference does it make how much I spent? You're paying for it."

One evening I ran into a gifted young poet, a boy I'd met once or twice who'd always spurned film-writing jobs as beneath his genius. He was seedy, threadbare, and he looked as though a meal wouldn't hurt either. I asked him to join me at the Café Hungaria, one of the best restaurants in town.

"Not if you're going to ask me to work," he told me.

"I won't. I promise."

The waiter gave us the menus and I ordered first: roast pork. The poet took his time, finally deciding on roast young gosling, a *specialité de la maison* and priced accordingly.

"They've got other things here too," I said. "I ordered pork. You don't have to go overboard."

The poet regarded me with no little annoyance. "Why shouldn't I have the gosling?" he said. "How often do I get a chance to eat in a restaurant like this?"

Some people regard this sort of thing as indicating a lack of principle. But they do the Hungarians a great injustice. They make the mistake of attempting to impose on them a foreign set of values. As well expect a Boston banker to urge dipping into capital for a week at Las Vegas as to think a Hungarian should be squeamish about taking what by pure chance belongs not to him but to a friend.

To the proper Budapestian what was mine was his. The most perfect such was a gentleman who now resides in my immediate neighborhood. Time and our wonderful country have dealt kindly with him. He has several respectable bank accounts, a portfolio of good investments and a closetful of annuities, and has become insufferably dull. But at the time of which I write he was undented by contact with money, except as he was able to borrow it. Lest his present standing as a triple-A credit risk be endangered by talk of his amiable past, let's identify him only as Laci.

I was Laci's pigeon. Before his charm, his pleas, his angles, his enormous persuasiveness, I was helpless. When I knew he was working me over, I could only admire his inventiveness, his rich imagination, and always, his boldness.

Once I moved to Vienna to shoot *Spring Parade*, a story with an Austrian background. I brought with me almost my whole technical staff. I stayed at the Imperial, a perfectly acceptable address, if not absolutely unexception-

143

able like, say, the Bristol. I felt, not to put too fine a point on it, that I could not afford the Bristol.

I was surprised by Laci in the lobby of the Imperial. I could not imagine where he'd raised the money for the fare from Budapest. "What're you doing in Vienna?" I asked him.

"How would I manage in Budapest when you're here?" he countered.

"What're you going to do with yourself?"

He shrugged. "I don't know. That's your problem."

"In that case, first get yourself a room somewhere. I've got a business appointment. I'll see you later."

He returned in time for dinner. I was not surprised. I expected him. "Where are you staying?" I asked him.

"The Bristol," he said offhandedly.

"The Bristol! I'm staying here because *I* can't afford the Bristol."

He put a hand on my shoulder to calm me. "Ten or twenty schillings more a day—what's the difference to you, Joe? I won't stay there forever."

"But the least you could do is to stay at some smaller hotel where they don't charge so much."

Laci shook his head at my obvious lack of understanding of how these things ran. "If I stay at a second-class hotel, what happens? I call for a bottle of wine or dinner, they expect to be paid. Right away. They have a middle-class mentality. But at the Bristol, I don't have to worry. I can sign to my heart's content—and they send the bill to you. There's no embarrassment, don't you understand?"

With marvelous Hungarian logic, Laci persuaded me that it was I who was wrong and he right.

144

"You can stay at the Imperial," he explained. "Everyone takes it as a sign that you're so wealthy you don't care where you stay. You're satisfying a whim. But if I don't stay at the Bristol, everybody looks at me and says, 'Look at that bum. He's down and out.' I can't afford to be poor."

A few days later Laci came to me and wanted to borrow fifty schillings. (They always call it *borrow*. This is where principle came in. They would never call it a *gift* or a *handout*: to have accepted either of these would have been beneath them and a dreadful blow to their pride. On the other hand, it was not necessary to pay back unless they got rich themselves. *Rich,* by the way, in Hungarian can be roughly defined as having enough money for next month's rent.)

I knew I was dead, of course, when Laci asked for the fifty schillings, but I wanted to get in the act. "What for?" I said.

"Don't ask me, please." His hand touched his heart. "I need it. That's all."

"Surely I have a right to know why?"

"Just because it's your money?"

I had wounded his pride. "Still," I offered plaintively, almost apologizing. "I'd like to know what you're going to do with it."

"I've never lied to you, Joe, and I won't begin now. I can't tell you and I need the money. Enough?"

Naturally I had visions of a secret tryst with some bigwig's mistress, heaven-knows-what romantic intrigue. I shelled out.

An hour later he was back, sporting a handsome Homburg, an American Stetson, as he proudly showed me. "You like it?" he asked eagerly.

"You borrowed my money for that?"

"Of course. Isn't it a beauty?"

"*I* don't wear a hat that expensive," I said irritatedly.

"You don't have to. Everybody knows you have money. The trouble with you," he broke off to explain, "is that you don't understand how the poor people of this world must live."

On completion of *Spring Parade,* we all went back to Budapest. In contrast with dull, spent Vienna, Budapest appeared to me more charming than ever.

My last night in Budapest is worth describing, for by itself it tells almost everything about my feeling for that lovely city. About twenty-five of the Old Guard gathered at the Parisian Grill, men and women, it ought to go without saying, for what good would a party be without lovely women? The Hungarian pledges his love and loyalty with a wineglass no one else may touch, so our party was punctuated with the joyful tinkle of crystal champagne glasses crashing against the wall. One of the men even refused to permit the mirror behind the bar to gaze again at any party so gay and touching, so he smashed that too.

But the Parisian Grill wasn't the only restaurant in town that had to be said goodbye to. We left—there were now some thirty-five of us—for a last touch of the wine cellar at the Hungaria. The gypsy musicians and the head-waiter, who fell into the mood of things, came along. Taxis wouldn't do, of course, so eight or nine fiacres were hired to take us all to the next stop. As we clip-clopped down

146

the cold January streets, strangers opened their windows and waved us farewell. The gypsies played, despite the jouncing of the carriages and the cold that bit into their fingers.

At the Hungaria there was more glass-breaking and more friends to drink to and to weep with and another group of gypsies to make the ride to the Café New York more agreeable. This went on from establishment to establishment until five, when, champagne-logged and arm-weary from raising my arm in so many toasts, I had only one wish: to sleep before my train left at eight-thirty. My hosts, gracious as always, bedded me down at the Royale, where I had once had a suite before I took a house. There, stationing my chauffeur Elemer and another husky character, unknown to me, at the outer door, they let me sleep.

I woke up at eight. Outside my door the gypsies were still playing softly. I got into my trousers and discovered someone had thoughtfully divested me of some 200 pengoes, about forty American dollars. I knew it was not Elemer and I had no wish to embarrass the stranger stationed to watch over me. But some of this money, which would be worthless to me in a few hours and which I meant to hand out anyway before I left to Elemer and some others, ought, I thought, go to the people it was intended for.

I called Elemer in. A true Hungarian, he was not troubled at the immorality of the theft, rather distressed by its ungraciousness. He had a few words alone with the culprit and brought him in to see me.

"I'm sorry," he said. "I knew you were going away and I didn't want the money to go to waste."

"I intended to give it out," I explained.

"I just thought I'd save you the trouble."

"Thanks, but give half of it to Elemer, will you?"

When it came time to leave for the station, all the gypsies were ranged down the big staircase to the main lounge, and the staff of the hotel, from the *sommelier* to the porters and the bootblacks and the chambermaids and the kitchen help were lined up in the lobby. Not one of them would accept a gratuity, though I tried to force a tip here and there. When I tell you the Hungarian attitude toward money is crazy and wonderful, this may help convince you.

In the cold winter morning they brought me to the station. Now a dozen schoolboys danced behind the gypsies. I looked out from the train window at my assembled friends. The musicians had now attracted a crowd so big that it included many people I did not even know. I saw one face lifted in song, the eyes bright, for they belonged to a man who was never so happy as when he was in love or making music. His name was Imre Harmath, in my considered opinion one of the three wittiest, cleverest, most charming lyricists of our time, which means that I rank him with Larry Hart and Ira Gershwin.

I have never forgotten that face, for somehow it symbolizes all that I cherish in the Hungarians. Imre is gone now, murdered during the twelve-year madness of the German people. Perhaps it is just as well. For I do not doubt that the new masters of Hungary would fail to appreciate his priceless spirit as much as did the exponents of the Master Race.

Imre was a true gypsy. If he had enough money in his pockets for dinner, for a bauble for a girl he had fallen in love with (he was always falling madly in love), he would not work though the skies might fall. He was a gypsy and also a real Hungarian and he believed one did not work for the pleasure of it. Nor did a man work for money if he had a few bills in his wallet. To tell him that he might need the money tomorrow or the day after brought forth the classic *zigeuner* reply: "I'll worry about that tomorrow."

The only time Imre ever completed a score on schedule was when he and Nicky promoted me into an advance to send them to a spa on the Adriatic. I knew I was being taken, nor did I mind. (Nicky said I was a fool not to join them, which I was.)

Nicky has told me since then that he and Imre had the whole score ready before the train crossed the Hungarian frontier. Why? They were determined to have fun on the Adriatic and they didn't want the prospect of work to dim it.

On another occasion Imre needed money fast. He had been refusing to get down to work and write the lyrics for a song for me, always pleading he was busy with a beautiful girl and couldn't spare the time. On this occasion he was flat broke, luckily for me.

He promised that if I gave him the money he would deliver the lyrics.

But I had done this before and he had let me down. I wasn't resentful, mind; I was realistic. As Imre himself explained to me, once he had the money, how could I imagine he'd work?

So I made a deal with him. I locked him, with Nicky, in a room with a piano. As he turned out the lyrics I paid him so much a line, cash on the line, so to speak. I sat in an adjoining room and as Imre finished each verse, he would toss it through the transom and I, in turn, would let the money flutter down to him. The arrangement worked perfectly too, until Imre had exactly the cash he needed.

As I say, Imre is gone, a fellow of infinite jest, of most excellent fancy. In a way he is a symbol of a whole mode of living—of music, funmaking, and lovemaking that was strange and wonderful.

Perhaps the new masters of Hungary see in the Budapest I knew and loved an example of bourgeois decay and corruption. They are as humorless as the domestic and German Nazis who murdered this charming fellow. With Imre has gone a whole way of life. So even now I remember him waving goodbye to me, his voice unheard through the train window, but the music in his face was just the same. I do not weep for him, for I have greater and more personal reasons to weep at what the Nazis did to me and to my people. But even today we can be sorry that the life we knew then is gone. There is nothing quite like it left in all the world now, and we are poorer for it, believe me.

17. *Goodbye to All That*

It had been obvious, of course, even when I was happily making pictures in Budapest, that the sands were running out in Central Europe. Laemmle asked me to go to London to look over the ground there. He asked me to consider transferring our movie making to England.

I intend no slight to London, a city which has always been a pleasant host to me. But it was not Budapest. Need one say more? I had scarcely checked into Claridge's when the first words of my negative report were being framed in my head. It simply did not seem to be a spot where I could operate as I had in Berlin or Budapest.

And yet I knew I must begin to think about leaving Europe.

The main reason I wanted to go home to America was that I was plagued with the feeling that the parade had passed me by. They had in fact forgotten all about me in Hollywood. I had been away too long—eight years in all. People at home had forgotten I was an American. As far as they were concerned, I was a European who had visited the States for a while.

Meanwhile it was becoming more and more difficult to

make films anywhere in Europe. I was proud to be honored by being blacklisted by Hitler, so that when my pictures were shown in Germany my name had to be taken off. But each country, for reasons which I leave to the historians, raised difficulties about the transfer of moneys, about import and export licenses; they taxed this and they put imposts on that. Soon, I knew, history would catch up with me, as it would one day with the life I loved in Budapest, and I would be finished. Once again I would be jobless, forgotten, a stranger in a strange land.

In London I talked to Alex Korda and some of his associates. There were discreet hints (on both sides; by all means, let's be honest) about one day joining forces. My problem, simply, was this: I wanted to stay on in Budapest as long as I could, because I loved it. But I wanted to be sure of a chance to make a picture or two in Hollywood when I returned, so they could see what I was capable of doing.

It happened that in Budapest my office manager was a gentleman who believed it part of his fiscal duties to read my mail and otherwise apprise himself of all the details in the lives of the company's creative talent. He read and duly reported all to my superiors in Universal City.

I began to think how I could use this gentleman's excellent contacts.

I recalled that twice before in my life, at critical junctures, I had created a demand where none or little existed. I had sold *rezor* by sending in a bearded stranger to ask for it; I had got orders for an obscure toothpaste by making it seem that a huge market awaited any druggist who signed my order book.

When my father was drafted and I was installed as the *shammas* it seemed fitting that the new incumbent sit for his portrait.

It didn't take long after I started in the picture business to develop a careless professional slouch.

This is how I looked when I first started, however. *That* day, I think, they let me be an assistant cameraman.

Above: Franciska Gaal, when we worked together in Germany, at the height of her success abroad.

Left: I like this photo of Marlene I've always kept. Somehow it is all the things she was and would become.

I've got my hand on Nicky Brodszky's shoulder, the late Felix
Bressart is doing what actors like to do, and do so well, which
is taking a bow, and Bobby Koster and Franciska Gaal are
holding hands. The occasion: a very lavish première in Berlin.

I don't remember any of these people, nor even the title of the picture we were making in the snow. But I do recall that we had a lot of fun on location.

That would be Wesley Ruggles in the director's chair and his
assistant beside the camera. It being the time of silent pictures
(before I went to Germany) the musicians had to be there, of
course—even at the waterfront.

Deanna Durbin when she started working with Leopold Stokowski. The man in the monocle was her coach, André de Segurola.

Photo by Herbert Dallinger

The Koster-Pasternak team was always talking things over between shots wherever there was a corner of the set where we could be, more or less, alone.

Deanna and her producer were given some honor—again my memory fails as to just when and why—and we both were more thrilled than when the reports of the business her pictures were doing came in.

Photo by Roman Freulich

Bobby likes a close-up position when he directs. Here he is
with Stoki and Adolphe Menjou when we made *One Hundred
Men and a Girl*. My hand is on the late Joe Valentine, the
cameraman. Incidentally, his assistant, the operating cameraman, is Robert Surtees, today acknowledged one of the finest
cameramen in the film world.

Photo by Bill Dudas

Jimmy, Lauritz and José at a party in my old house.

Photo by Roman Freulich

Shirley Temple wrote me once that her ambition was to meet Deanna. Instead of tea, this is what Deanna served.

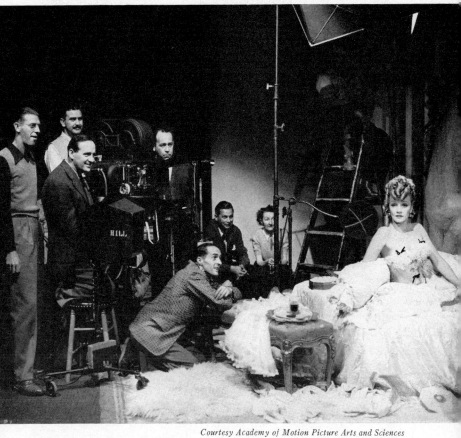

René Clair working with Marlene in *The Flame of New Orleans*. Just behind him is the cameraman, Rudy Maté, now a director.

Patricia Medina, Jimmy Durante and Mario Lanza tuning up
with the producer at a set party after we completed one of our
pictures.

With Jack Benny, Louella Parsons and Lily Pons at an award
dinner.

Her name is Joan Fay Brown and she was the telephone girl at Dick Pope's Cypress Gardens—*was,* until I decided she belonged in pictures.

When Szakall came to America, I gave a party to introduce him to everyone I knew.

Lana Turner and I have made a couple of pictures together. I hope we get to make at least a couple more.

Above: The fun of being a producer comes when you get to stand in the middle of a bouquet of long-stemmed American Beauties.

Left: Every so often I still get ambitious enough to make Chicken Pasternak. Here's Jane Powell on one of those days.

Photo by William Read Woodfield

Dorothy, with Michael and Jeffrey, some years ago.

Sunday is a frantic day around our house with the three boys, but do you know what? I love it.

With Korda I found my chance. I trust that Alex will forgive me, but, well-lubricated by several bottles of Mumm Brut 1928, one of his emissaries, who must obviously remain nameless, agreed to play a joke on my office manager, this fellow who had the effrontery to steam open my letters. I persuaded him to send a letter to my office in Budapest begging me to join forces with Korda for two years at a substantial salary. The letter was dispatched before I left London, so news of it would reach Hollywood even as I returned to Budapest.

Sure enough, two weeks after my return from London, I found a cable from Carl Laemmle one morning. I was offered the same deal Korda had supposedly advanced.

There was one more string to my bow. I wanted Henry Koster to come along.

I wired this to Laemmle. CAN KOSTER SPEAK LANGUAGE? he cabled back. The answer was an unequivocal no, if Uncle Carl was referring to English, as he undoubtedly was. HE READS AND WRITES PERFECTLY, I informed Laemmle. I meant German, of course, but I had no doubt someone might think we were talking about English. I hoped so, anyway. Oh, the things a man will do for a talented pal!

Anyway, a contract for one year was offered to Koster and a two-year contract was in my vault. Now I was willing to stay in Europe as long as the brass wanted me there.

Still, it was not to be for long. Our markets were closing down. Our pictures were better than ever, in my opinion, but, frightened by what was happening in Europe, the statesmen hastened toward self-destruction. The tariff walls betweens the nations of Europe were going higher and higher.

One day the cable I knew must come did come: ON COMPLETION PRESENT PRODUCTION YOU ARE ORDERED TO CEASE ALL PRODUCTION IN EUROPE AND RETURN TO AMERICA.

One thing remained to be done.

I went home to see my father. My mother had passed on a few years before. I had the gratification of knowing that everything possible had been done for her. I wanted my father and my sister Helen, her husband, and her children to come to America.

My father was growing older but he was still strong. He was still proud to serve as *shammas* of the synagogue and to supervise the ritual functions of the whole community.

I tried to tell him what I'd seen in Germany. I voiced my fears about the impending war. "Come to America, father," I said, "and make a new life."

"Your grandmother, my mother, is still alive," he told me. "The commandment says one must honor his father and mother. If I left her now, in her old age, would that be honoring her? No, I must stay near her."

"Maybe we can bring her too," I offered.

He shook his head. "Besides, if I did not go years ago, would it not be foolish now, when I am so much older? I belong here. These are my people, this is my town, my congregation, my world. When I have visited you in Budapest, I have found the ways strange. I do not say they are wrong and I do not blame you. But I have grown too old to grow new roots. And, also, my son, I love it here. Do not be harsh on me for wanting to remain."

My sister Helen, the only one of the children who had not left home, felt she must stay too. She had her own family now, and also she knew that if she left, my father, who loved his family so much, would feel utterly lost. "Do not ask me to go," she begged me.

As he had done years before, my father took me to the station. It was the same train and it left at the same hour in the middle of the night. In the dark the years seemed to have touched my father lightly. We both knew that the likelihood of seeing each other again was very slim. My father did not say much. For my part, when I tried to speak, the words would not come out.

I have thought of our parting many, many times. I never saw my father again. He was alive when the war started, some years later. My remittances to him were always cashed, though I have good reason to doubt they ever reached him. He, my sister Helen, her husband, their six young children, and some forty-odd relatives of mine, as well as my old teacher Schwarz, were taken by the Germans during the war and destroyed in their murder camps. I am sure my father's last words, as were those of another great Jew, were a plea for forgiveness of his tormentors. He was that kind of man.

18. Return to Hollywood

FEBRUARY 24, 1936, must have been a dull day in the city rooms of the New York newspapers. A day or two before the Supreme Court had declared the TVA constitutional, but on the morning of my arrival back in this country there was little to write about. One story said that vast dust clouds were harassing the west. Another announced that Mongolia was to be taken under the Soviet wing. There was a delay in Congress in passing new tax measures. But right there, on page one, where by all the rules of history and journalism it scarcely belonged, William A. H. Birnie, then a reporter for the New York *World-Telegram,* found his copy:

EX-WAITER WHO KNEW WHAT STARS ATE TO MAKE "DIFFERENT" FILMS AS PRODUCER

Joe Pasternak, who is Hollywood-bound with a $500-a-week contract as associate producer for Universal, said today he got his start in life by knowing just what the stars wanted to eat.

"That was when I was a waiter out at the old Paramount studios on Long Island," he explained between sips of a cherry flip in his suite in the Hotel Algonquin.

"Why, they didn't even have to order! Gloria Swanson—lamb chops, dry. Bebe Daniels—chicken sandwich, no butter. Tom Meighan—Irish stew with plenty of salt.

"Say, if Gloria walked in here tomorrow, I think I'd jump up and say, 'Your chops'll be right up, Miss Swanson.'

If Miss Swanson did walk in, however, she wouldn't find her erstwhile waiter because he is leaving tomorrow for the coast where he dreams of making "different" pictures.

"It isn't just the money that makes me happy," he said. "It's the chance to contribute to the entertainment of humanity. No one's going to get sick or die in my pictures. That's no sort of entertainment."

There was a good deal more in that vein. However, even at this late date, I might as well file two minor disclaimers. I never had anything to do with anything called a cherry flip. Secondly, although I had a contract with Universal, I wasn't too sure about the welcome I could expect.

Yet the story served one useful purpose. It gave notice to the Hungarian colony in New York that a flush pigeon had flown into town. I spent two days listening to an endless parade of friends-of-friends, putative relatives, and the usual charming rascals. For the sake of my exchequer, preparing itself for buffeting in Hollywood, I hoped that some small revolution would break out in some banana republic so that news of my arrival in Hollywood would not alert too many compatriots.

I needn't have worried. Two fugitives, crossing an arroyo on a moonless night, could not have asked for a less conspicuous entrance into the City of the Angels. The town itself had grown visibly bigger and busier. When Bobby Koster and I presented ourselves at the Universal lot, it too seemed to have grown bigger. There were only a few people to greet me. Greg La Cava drove by, late and hurrying to a stage where the company was awaiting its director. He asked me to drop by. I didn't like the face he put on while talking to me. He seemed to know something I didn't.

No matter. Bobby and I bravely walked into Carl Laemmle's office. The old man's eyes twinkled brightly when he saw us. He greeted me warmly. Bobby he found enchanting, delighted at the opportunity to use his *geboren* German so much that he forgot to speak English.

He told us how proud he was of what we had done in Europe. He had made it a point to see all our pictures; they were delightful, they were this, they were that. I could hardly believe my ears. Then we were in good shape. Why had I let nameless fears assail me? He had big plans for us. Why didn't we take it easy for a while, kind of survey the ground, look around, acclimatize ourselves and then we'd talk again?

When we walked out of his office, Bobby and I felt lightheaded. It wasn't true, I felt, that the parade had passed me by. All the time the boss had known; no one had said anything. But, leave it to him: he had known.

We went over to see Greg, saturnine and cynical as always. I told him the wonderful news. Greg tugged me by the lapel and brought me into comparative privacy behind the stand of an arc lamp.

"Don't kid yourself," he said. "He may not even own this studio tomorrow. He's been dickering with an Eastern syndicate for months. Besides, his son Junior's running this joint now and if there's one thing the kid can't stand it's 'great' European producers and directors."

"But I'm not a European," I protested. "I'm an American."

"To them you're a European. Just don't be surprised what happens. And whatever you do, for heaven's sake, be tough."

Greg knew what he was talking about. Two days later it was announced that the studio with all its assets, liabilities, and obligations, had been bought by an Eastern syndicate headed by Charles R. Rogers. The new management made the usual statements about new brooms, dead wood, and reorganization.

Bobby, who had a contract for one year with a layoff term optional to the studio for thirteen weeks, was immediately put on layoff.

When I spoke to the studio manager about an office, that gentleman hinted that since I would be leaving in a day or so, it hardly seemed worth the trouble.

Undiscouraged, Bobby and I presented ourselves at the studio gate every morning. No office and no duties. Outside of Greg, nobody on the lot even cared to acknowledge us. But I was determined not to give the new management a lever to discharge me by claiming that I did not show up for work and hence had breached the contract myself.

Even the gateman did not know us. Every morning Bobby and I would show up at the Main Gate. The following scene repeated itself with a deadly repetitiousness:

GATEMAN: Hey, there, you can't go on the lot without a pass.

ME: Yes, I can. I'm a producer here.

GATEMAN: Y'are? What's your name?

ME: Pasternak, Joe Pasternak.

GATEMAN (after duly searching through all his lists): We got nobody by that name here.

ME: We just started here. This is my director, Henry Koster.

GATEMAN: Sorry. You can't get in.

ME: Call the front office and ask them.

GATEMAN (reluctantly): All right, all right.

To use the theatrical locution, we got the business in every style, shape, and form. Bobby and I, without an office to hide in, took to whiling the day away in the shade of various live oaks around the premises. It always happened that we were no sooner settled than a gardener would turn on the sprinklers all around us.

Koster and I debated the advisability of returning to Europe. There were some powerful arguments in its favor. I knew I could make some kind of deal with Alex Korda in England. I could certainly return to Budapest and raise all the capital I needed. But it went against my grain to run from the kind of treatment I was getting.

Edward Muhl, who now heads Universal-International, and was then, I suppose, assigned the job by the company, called me into his office for what I'm sure he hoped

—for his sake as well as mine—would be a mercifully brief decapitation.

"You know," he began, "that Mr. Laemmle is no longer boss here. You fellows are through. Naturally, we understand you've incurred a little expense coming all this way from Europe. We're prepared to give you a few hundred dollars, just to show you our heart's in the right place."

"Well, that's very kind of you," I told Ed, "and I don't want you to think I don't appreciate it. I do. Truly. But I thing I'll stay here."

"Well, of course that's your privilege. But you won't be working for us."

"You think so? I've got a contract. It isn't with Carl Laemmle. It's with Universal. That means the new management. If I have to hire a bunch of lawyers to read the contract to tell me what I know it says, I'll do it."

"Oh, no, no, Joe," he said, affably. "There's no question you have a contract." He tried the man-to-man, friendly approach. Why get legal about all this? We were friends-among-friends, weren't we? Here was this new management, so anxious to make a fresh start, so virginal, so pure; who but a louse would not wish them well? Who would want to saddle the shining infant management with a bunch of old obligations? They were reasonable, nice guys. We were all reasonable, nice guys, right? Why couldn't we sit down and come to a reasonable settlement, a few thousand maybe that could help me get started again?

I got to my feet. I didn't want a settlement. I wanted to do the job I was hired to do. I'd remained in Europe for almost eight years more than I went over for in the first place because they'd said I could make pictures in America eventually. If they wouldn't let me work, which was their right, they'd have to pay me. I'd take every penny I had coming to me right now, in advance.

I knew some fiscal facts of life myself, and I felt pretty sure the new management had lots of everything except cash.

A few days later, I was informed office space had been provided for Koster and Pasternak. The "office" turned out to be four bare walls, in a barnlike structure that has since been remodeled to be the gymnasium on the Universal-International lot. Right next to it a number of horses were stabled. Our meditations and crap games were frequently interrupted by strange stampings and whinnyings and often when the wind shifted in the late afternoon we had trouble reminding ourselves that we were in a motion picture studio, but Bobby and I were happy. Such as it was, we had achieved our first foothold in Hollywood.

The secretary who presented herself to me sniffed curiously as she came into our quarters. She was pretty, gave an appearance of being competent—and almost two decades later I have never had an occasion to deny this. Like most good secretaries, she came to be our best source of information about this and that around the lot. Eleanor Lewis cheered us when we were blue; she believed in us when we doubted our ability; and she urged us to be strong when we wanted to run for cover.

One morning when we arrived for work, Eleanor announced: "The boss wants to see you." That would be

Charley Rogers. "I guess you know what he'll ask?" Bobby and I both shook our heads, incredulous still about the news. "A story, of course. You'd better be prepared with *some*thing."

On the way to Rogers' office Bobby and I tried to come up with something that might sound plausible. The fact is that we'd been so busy fighting to get a toe inside the studio door that we had neglected to prepare ourselves with anything positive once we had been admitted.

"What are we going to do?" I asked Bobby, worried.

"Tell him we want to do a story about a girl."

"A girl. That's good. People always like a story about a girl. Maybe two girls. Maybe that's better?"

"What about *three* girls? Not just any girls. But smart girls. Three smart girls."

We were at Rogers' door. "That's fine."

To my worried eyes, Rogers looked like a tough police lieutenant about to question a thief he's caught red-handed with the goods. If I do a fine man an injustice, I do not mean it; blame it on my insecurity at the time.

"Well, boys," he greeted us, "what would you like to do?"

"We're picture makers," I said, stalling for time, hoping to give the brilliant, fertile imagination I knew Koster possessed time to come up with a story about those three girls. "We've got a title. *Three Smart Girls*."

Rogers played with it briefly. "I like it," he concluded crisply. "What's the story?"

"Tell Mr. Rogers, Bobby," I said, giving Bobby my best imitation of an innocent face.

Bobby was still very new in the English language and

163

I let him talk. I realized that Rogers was having as much difficulty making out what he was hearing as he was understanding the elements in the story Bobby was proposing.

Finally, I broke in. "You get the idea. Why don't we get it down on paper for you and then you can see what it's like?"

"All right. Good." Rogers was visibly relieved.

So were we. We had a picture to make, even if we didn't know what the story would be.

19. Deanna

SOME weeks after our interview with Rogers, we got the go-ahead on the script of *Three Smart Girls*. For a time after our arrival at the studio Bobby and I had thought that our troubles would be over if only we could get a picture to do. Now we found that they had just begun. We had a script and approval to shoot it, but who was going to play the leading role?

What we dreamed of, Bobby and I, was a young Mary Pickford. The only way this would ever happen, I realized, was for a fairy godmother to touch us with her wand. There didn't seem to be any fairy godmothers around the Universal lot. I was feeling pretty blue. First, we'd arrived and had been told we were fired. I fought that and won. Then we had to live in an atmosphere where nobody believed we could work up an acceptable shooting script. We got one ready and it was accepted. And what did we find? We needed a twelve-year-old girl with the indefinable charm of the girl who was once rightly called America's sweetheart. That's all.

The plain fact was, everybody told us, there was no such creature. Bobby and I talked over the possibilities. Dejected, we decided we'd have to change the story and make it about a twelve-year-old boy. We both grimaced at the title. *Three Smart Boys.* For some reason it sounded ridiculous. "Why don't we go back to Europe?" Bobby muttered. "We never had such troubles there."

"Don't worry. Something will turn up."

Sure enough, it did. We found a benefactor in the person of the late Rufus Le Maire, who had just come over to Universal as casting director after many years of service at Metro-Goldwyn-Mayer. I called on him and told him our problem.

Rufus grinned. "I think I know just where to find such a girl. In fact, you can have your choice of two."

"Choice?" My voice cracked. Here I was, asking for another Mary Pickford and this man says there are more than one.

"Over at Metro they've got two kids under contract. They both have tremendous possibilities, I think. I'll get the film and run it for you. I'm pretty sure they're dropping one of them."

I could hardly wait until the next day when the film arrived. Everything Rufus said was right. The girl was warm, lovable, natural, charming. She sang in a way to win your heart.

"That's the girl," I shouted when the light went up in the projection room. "What do you say, Bobby?"

Bobby agreed. We turned, beaming huge smiles at Rufus. He kept swallowing, staring at us, unable to make a word come out of his mouth. "What's the matter, Rufus?" I said. "Don't you understand? We like her, she's terrific. You can sign her."

166

A thin stream of words finally came out of Rufus. "Remember I told you they had two girls and were dropping one? *This* is the one they decided to keep."

I fell into a chair and covered my face with the palms of both hands. Rufus came up to us, his voice found, determined to cheer us up. "She's pretty good, this kid, huh, Joe? Her name's Garland, Judy Garland. I knew you'd like her."

"Rufus, will you for heaven's sake stop? What do I care if her name's Fifi LaFlamme? If I can't have her for my picture, what difference does it make?"

"This other kid's good too. Let me ask the projectionist to run her film too."

"What's the use, Rufus? It's bad enough looking for one as good as that, and finding her. There aren't two—not in the same generation."

"I think this other kid's great too, Joe. You're here—you might as well look." Rufus gave the signal to the booth.

This was a singing test, but the moment the girl's face was flashed on the screen Bobby and I sat up. Bobby was sitting in the seat immediately behind me. He didn't say a word, just leaned forward and put his hand on my shoulder. The girl had a sweetness without being arch or cloying; she was natural; she was pretty; she was wholesome; and she sang beautifully with a skill and ability far beyond her years.

When the lights went up again, Bobby and I couldn't say a word. Rufus stood before us. "Before I say anything, is this girl free, can we sign her?" I demanded of him.

Rufus nodded.

"Can she act?" Bobby asked. "All we've seen here is singing. I don't care—" Bobby went on, not waiting to hear the answer—"I'll teach her to act. She's wonderful." Bobby and I threw arms around each other.

Holding her mother's hand, Deanna Durbin came to the studio, shy, timid, scarcely willing, or able, to utter a word. We knew she could sing beautifully because of her test. She had had some experience in radio, one or two guest shots, so we also knew she was a performer, however green. She wore a simple cotton dress that came to her knees, white socks, Mary Janes. Her hair was long, brushed out. Bobby and I were pleasantly surprised to find her even prettier than her screen test had indicated. We knew that with a top-flight cameraman, such as we would insist on, audiences would find her as beautiful as she was. We would always see to that.

Because of her shyness and inexperience, we decided that Bobby should spend a week or two coaching her privately at his home. He reported that she was coming along beautifully. All she needed was confidence.

No one makes a star, of course; not the producer, not the director, not the writer. It is a matter of chemistry between the public and the player, and the player must come to the public, just as the public must come to the player to make her a star. Deanna's genius had to be unfolded; but it was hers alone, always was, and no one "discovered" her or can take credit for her. You can't hide that kind of light under a bushel. You just can't, even if you try.

We knew Deanna was great from the time we saw the

first rushes. But we had our problems. On the lot we were still dubbed the "*shammas* outfit." We were not regarded as pros in a business where there is no time or inclination for amateurs. We were holdovers from the old management. It was an open secret that the studio, stuck with our contracts, was letting us make this one picture just to get some work for all the money they were condemned to pay us. It was widely bruited about that after the flop which was sure to take place, we would be given our walking papers, contract or no contract.

Naturally, there were also the theatrical know-it-alls, who flutter about the edges of every enterprise. They knew that the public hated child actors at what they assured us was "the awkward age." Shirley Temple was different. She was a mere child. But a girl of twelve! She was nothing, neither child nor woman.

Because of Bobby's still limited English, the studio management assigned a dialogue director to the picture. It was his job to make sure the lines were read in a natural American way. But every time Bobby finished a scene we turned to find the dialogue director shaking his head. Bobby and I exchanged panicked looks. The dialogue sounded good to us, real, natural, believable. But maybe we could be wrong? I'd been away so long, maybe I didn't have the common touch? The dialogue director kept shaking his head disapprovingly. Nothing Bobby did seemed to please him.

Finally I decided to find out for myself why the dialogue director didn't like anything. Soon I discovered the reason.

"You know what?" I reported to Bobby later. "He

169

shakes his head because he's got a nervous tic. He loves what you're doing."

Other problems involved integrating music into our story. For example, when someone played a piano and Deanna started to sing, we had an orchestra come in behind her. It was an old, proved device to us, as I have said, for René Clair had used it in his films and we had all proved in countless pictures in Europe that no one minds.

But some of the production people still said it was wrong. "Couldn't we have a band passing under her window?" they said. "Where does the music come from?"

"That would be a coincidence," I insisted. "The music comes from the heart, so everybody hears it."

Deanna was the girl who could sing from the heart, no question. While we were making the picture, she started to sing regularly on Eddie Cantor's radio program. Eddie Cantor must, of course, be given full marks for first bringing Deanna's voice to the world on the radio. He heard her when she was an unknown and shared the thrill of his discovery with the vast radio audience.

During the shooting of the picture, Deanna was frightened. And so were Bobby and I. In fact, it doesn't take much sharpness to figure out why she was frightened. She caught it from the producer and the director. One morning Bobby was shooting a scene with Charley Winninger. The action called for Charley to sit abruptly on the piano keyboard. Charley did it a dozen times, each time, however, anticipating his reaction before he actually touched the keys. Bobby had to take the scene over and over, patiently explaining to Charley that first he must hit the notes and then respond. Bobby was ready to try it again when from the darkness of the stage we heard an imperious: "That's enough! No more!"

It came from one of the studio's top executives, a gentleman who has since passed away so I will preserve his anonymity out of decent respect. He strode forward to the camera and the set. "You're wasting the company's money. Who cares if he's a second fast in his reaction? You're not in Europe now, you're in America!"

We had our choice then and there: knuckling down or returning to Europe, after all our troubles getting started. Well, we're here, so our decision is fairly obvious. Protest didn't do us much good on that first picture, but Bobby and I resolved that if we came up with a hit, we'd never let a thing like that happen to us again.

I knew we had a good picture when I saw the first rough cut. All the lack of confidence I ran into around the studio had undercut my own confidence a little (I've never let it happen since) so I wasn't sure that *Three Smart Girls* would be a hit. But Bobby and I were sure that if we had made this picture in Hungarian and German, we would have come up with a successful picture.

How the American audiences would take it, we didn't know. Around the lot the general feeling was that the music was too "highbrow." But we felt Deanna sang so simply, so beautifully, that she wiped out all distinction between "popular" and "serious" music, which is as it should be.

Well, the picture was successful beyond our fondest dreams. Naturally, Bobby and I were assigned at once to do another "Durbin picture," as they came to be called. We came up with a story about the daughter of an unemployed, down-at-heels musician who gets Leopold Stokowski to conduct a symphony orchestra composed of unemployed musicians.

Deanna was superb. I am theatrical enough to appreciate temperament. Do not consider temperament a failing among the people of stage and screen. Heaven save us from the day when the players of the make-believe world are as even-dispositioned as bearings-inspectors on an assembly line. (And who says they *don't* have temperament?) Winning confidence in herself, getting to know her *métier* as an artist must, demanding the perfection from her co-workers she must have so she herself could do her own best—these marked the emergence of our girl into a real star.

And we never again gave Deanna, or anyone else, cause to be afraid, or to doubt that we were fully responsible for the pictures we made. The next time the gentleman who had interrupted the scene with Charley Winninger came on the set, he said not a word and kept mouse-quiet, like any other visitor. That gave me all the satisfaction—or "revenge," if you like—I ever needed. I knew why he was keeping that quiet and he knew I knew. It was enough for both of us.

I had approached Stokowski with a certain amount of timidity, as I shall relate somewhat more fully later. You can imagine my consternation at a rehearsal one day when I heard Deanna break off her singing sharply and announce to the great conductor in firm, unshaken tones: "You're not doing it right, Mister Stokowski!"

Stoki waved his hands for the orchestra to stop. A terrible hush descended on the players and everybody else on the recording stage. I moved up discreetly to be handy when the full weight of the maestro's anger fell on the child.

Stoki descended from the podium and walked toward Deanna.

"*How* am I not doing it right?" he demanded coolly.

"It's just not right," Deanna said.

"Oh, it isn't, is it?"

"No." Just *no*. Not *sir*, not *maestro*. Just *no*. I had dizzying visions of the whole picture falling apart, of Stokowski walking off, refusing to have anything to do with a thirteen-year-old child who dared tell him about music.

But Stoki smiled suddenly. "Tell me how you would like it done, my dear," he said simply. He was big enough so he didn't have to fear losing face by accommodating himself to Deanna. I've always taken this episode as a sign of their common greatness: Stoki, who wasn't afraid to listen to a young girl, and Deanna, who already knew what was right for her and insisted on doing it that way even if it meant taking on the conductor of the Philadelphia Orchestra.

Deanna was learning how to be a movie star. Of course there are movie stars and movie stars. And when I say Deanna was learning to be one, what I mean was that she was learning how to project herself. This was an important step in her development as an actress and I was delighted to see it happen.

Once I got a call from a troubled assistant on the recording stage. Deanna and a big studio orchestra had been working all morning and the girl hadn't got a single song right. The costs were mounting up horribly.

The rain was coming down in the proverbial buckets, as it does in Southern California when it decides to rain. I got to the recording stage to find Deanna sitting alone in a corner, wretched and spiritless.

"Are you all right, Deanna darling?" I asked her. "You haven't got a headache or something?"

"No. I feel sad. All that rain."

"That's outside, dear. It's nice in here."

"I don't feel like singing when it's raining."

It was easier to call off the recording session than the rain, so I ordered the former. Besides, I was secretly pleased. My star was showing some "temperament."

But Deanna never did show to me the wild moods and flashes of temperament of many stars, most of whom have never even begun to achieve the greatness that she won with the public at the box office. Her pictures were responsible for transforming a studio then suffering from repeated attacks of passed dividends, nervous bankers, and changes of management, and putting it into a healthy, sound condition. Instead of bankruptcy, Universal faced a bright future. Our salesmen could sell (in those days of block-booking this was permissible) the studio's product simply by promising to deliver to the exhibitor a certain number of Deanna's pictures.

Did this have its effect on the character of the young, still growing girl? Did she become insufferable, conceited, spoiled? Did she make life intolerable for the grown-ups around her? The answer is a flat and absolute negative.

When I worked with her, she simply didn't know that hard-headed bankers and businessmen traded in shares of Universal Pictures, Inc., because of her; that people by the tens of thousands depended on her for a living. She was in every way a healthy, normal child, who happened also to be a movie star. There was only one matter in which she insisted on having her own way. I discovered to my horror one morning that my star's breakfast consisted of French fried potatoes liberally doused with ketchup. If she'd insisted on having Algerian strawberries flown in by chartered airplane, it would have been something I could appreciate. But French fries and ketchup! It was—well, it was un-starlike. I absolutely put my foot down. Besides, I insisted, it was bad for her digestion and her figure.

She was equally firm. "No French fries and ketchup for breakfast, no work."

P.S. As long as I knew her, Deanna had French fries and ketchup to start off the day. I still shudder a little at the thought, however.

It was my idea that Deanna would be an example for every girl to look up to. She would be dressed as a girl of her years should dress. Her growth would not be forced. I knew that some of our greatest actresses were playing adult roles by the time they were sixteen, but I didn't want this for Deanna. When she was sixteen, she would play parts suitable for a girl of that age.

After all, the difference is that the public knew Deanna from childhood, watched her, copied her, and identified itself with her. The mail that crossed my desk in bagfuls always pleaded that she be kept sweet and natural. There were the others, but they were mostly professionals, and I felt, to put it simply and bluntly, they were wrong.

Deanna herself went out hardly at all. Her birthdays were occasions for simple parties. She was considerate and respectful of her parents. And they, for their part, let me handle her career as I felt she should be handled.

The one exception came when, to my surprise, I was called into the executive offices late one afternoon. I found this strange because several of our pictures had done exceedingly well at the box office, there was a new management at the head of the studio, and gone were the days when we were called the *"shammas* outfit." The bosses usually came to see me.

I arrived to find Deanna's father, with whom I had always had the warmest relationship, in obvious battle position beside a squad of corporation brass. Matty Fox, their spokesman, obviously embarrassed at the task, spoke haltingly, beating about a variety of bushes.

"Matty," I said, "I know it pains you, whatever you have to say, but why don't you just say it and get it over with? What's up?"

"Well, Joe, it's this." Matty coughed. "Mr. Durbin here has been on the set the last few days and—well, frankly, he thinks Bobby Koster is favoring the other people, and—well, he's not doing all he should for Deanna."

"You're kidding?" I said, looking around.

"No, Joe. That's the way Mr. Durbin feels." I could not help feeling sorry for Matty who, like myself, regarded the whole business as extremely distasteful.

Even Mr. Durbin, now that it had been aired, didn't seem happy about it.

"I think we've done fairly well by Deanna," I said. "There's no question that we've handled her well so far?" I looked around. No exception on that point. "As for the shots you speak of, I don't know what school you went to, Mr. Durbin. I'd like to go to it if all you have to do is watch a director work and be able to tell how a picture is going to look when it's cut."

"Oh, he didn't mean that," Matty interjected.

"Whatever he meant, it seems to me our relationship has been based on mutual esteem and respect, and if there's any question about slighting Deanna—"

"Oh it isn't that," Mr. Durbin said. He looked out abashed. "I'm sorry I brought it up."

Suddenly we all looked at each other and grinned. I put out my hand to Durbin. "What the devil, why can't we behave like movie stars now and then, especially since we've got the biggest one in the whole wide world?"

The only reason for recalling this isolated incident today is that it is, truly, the only one like it in five years of my association with the Durbins. As Deanna herself grew older we had our differences, but they were small and easily resolved. They were the kind you must expect among creative people working together to do the best job each knows how. They might have had to do with something as petty as which hat she should wear in a scene. I know this. Those difficulties were so trivial I cannot for the life of me even remember what they were today.

I had some differences with management first, and later

with Deanna, about her roles. I insisted that Deanna was one of those personalities which the world not only takes to its bosom but insists as regarding as its personal property. We dressed her, as I said, with great consideration for her position. The occasion of her first kiss was as significant to us, and, as it happened, to her audience, as must be the first kiss of any girl sixteen years old. We instituted a veritable *Gone With the Wind*–style search for the right boy. Robert Stack finally won it. A million words must have been written on the subject. I do not contend that there were not more weighty matters at the time. But it is proof, I think, of the interest that every stage of Deanna's development held for the world.

There was, as I started to say, a difference of opinion about what we should do. I remember one afternoon being braced by a party of exhibitors to permit Deanna to take a "sexy" role now and then.

"After all," they said, "isn't it smart to throw a change of pace? And she isn't a little girl any more. She's a young lady. She's not much younger than girls we see on our theatre screens every day playing love scenes."

"Not while I have anything to do with her pictures," I said. "I thing you're wrong. If you try, you'll do no one any good."

Deanna herself, as she grew older, began to grow restive. I can understand her point of view. She would go to the movies and see girls not much older than herself playing vixens and hussies. Some of the critical gentry, out of a perverseness which I quite appreciate because it certainly makes for better copy, called for an end to "sweetness and light." No nice girl wants to be considered "nice" anyway.

So Deanna champed at the bit. I did my best to persuade Deanna. I reminded her she was only sixteen or seventeen and that there would be many years in which she could play heartless wenches, if that was what she and the public wanted. But right now, I insisted, it would not work and I certainly would be no part of it.

Working with a great star, making a succession of successful pictures, it was inevitable that someone, some bookkeeping executive, would try to separate the elements that went into the team's pictures. Koster and I never gave it a thought, but some business genius in a front office conceived the idea that if they separated us they might be able to get twice as much for their money. Besides, just what was the producer contributing? He simply happened to bring along from Europe the director who was "responsible."

They assigned Bobby to do another picture for another producer and, to tell the truth, it brought on a painful sequence of events for us both. I could not help feeling that I was being cut off from my support, my team; yet I knew Bobby was too splendid a talent to limit himself to one *genre* of filmmaking and one producer. I may have felt that as time went on, we'd branch out. I don't know. I have to be honest since I am telling the story of my life. I was hurt that Bobby did not stay with us to direct the third and fourth Durbin pictures.

But if the accountants and the corporation Blackstones had any doubts about what the producer was contributing to the continued Durbin successes, they soon began to lose them. *Mad About Music* and *That Certain Age* not only were liked by the critics; the public supported them vigorously too. Since I am being honest here, I have to confess that my battered ego was well bolstered by this.

Nevertheless I learned a lesson. It was entirely proper and in the nature of things that Bobby Koster and I go our own ways. It hurt at the time, as these things often do, but it happened for the best. Koster, Deanna, and I made pictures together afterward, three more to be exact, right up to the last one, *It Started With Eve*.

By that time I had made up my mind to leave Universal; and Deanna, against the advice which I was asked for and truly gave, was married.

She was eighteen when talk of marriage first reached me. Her mother and I discussed it and I did not think it wise. "Of course she will marry some day, and maybe soon, but I don't think it ought to be now," I offered. "To the world outside the studio Deanna is the normal, healthy everyday girl, the charming kid next door. But has she ever had a real childhood? She's worked hard, really hard, during all the years that other girls play. You know what I think she misses? A chance to be a girl just like every other girl. She hasn't been able to do all those things because she was working. But marriage? Besides," I added, testily perhaps, "she's too young, she hasn't lived enough yet to be married. Why don't you let her travel for a year? Take her around the world. All she knows is Hollywood and the way to the studio. Give her a chance to see what other people are like."

But I wasn't convincing anybody. Since I was unable

to make a secret of my attitude toward her marriage, it was inevitable that Deanna's impending marriage would complicate our relationship.

Vaughn Paul was a second assistant director, a young man of great promise and evident ability, attractive, well-spoken. Actually, in every way he would make the ideal husband for Deanna. He came from a good family, worked hard, was young. The couple appeared to be very much in love.

But when Deanna came to my office and said that on her next picture why didn't we have her prospective bride-groom's brother, who was a cameraman, photograph her, I had to be very firm. I had made a promise after seeing her first test that the cameraman who photographed her would always be absolutely top-notch. Rudy Maté and Joe Valentine had always been entrusted with this task and they were both artists of the finest stature.

"I won't do it, Deanna," I said. "Not that I have anything against this man you suggest. I don't know him. He may be great. I simply won't take a chance, that's all."

On April 18, 1941, Deanna became Mrs. Vaughn Paul. It was a church wedding and the way it was handled indicates a good deal about her character. The church was not filled with film notables, as it could easily have been. Deanna invited all the people she had worked with in her five years in pictures. There were carpenters, electricians, sound and camera men, grips and gaffers. The publicity department, with its usual cold heart, wanted pictures for the press of the world (the *New York Times* and the New York *Herald Tribune* correspondents both wired back long stories and wirephotos in appreciation of the news value of the event) but Deanna insisted there would be no movie hoopla. She was married beautifully and quietly, and I'd be a liar if I didn't own there were tears in my eyes.

When she returned from her honeymoon, we started our last picture together, *It Started With Eve*. By this time I knew I was leaving the studio. Deanna did not know. I called her into my office and told her why it had to be and why I was leaving.

It was the only time in our years together I saw her weep. "You can't," she said. "You can't do this to me."

But I had my personal reasons, and they did not all concern her and I said I must. It was not easy to talk to her because a lot of water had flowed under the bridge. She had her life to live now and it could not be the same as before. She said some nice things and ran out of the office.

I did not see her again for three years. By this time she had had a baby, been divorced, and had married my old friend Felix Jackson. We had a pleasant evening, talking about everything in the world except the past and pictures and ourselves.

And then I did not see her for a long time once more. At last, when I saw her, she had found happiness. She had married once again, for she had found herself, and when I saw her she was radiant, beautiful, glowing with the youthful charm which she always possessed. She is now married to Charles David, a French director, she lives in France, and she is really happy.

When she came to America the last time, the papers were full of gossip that she and I would make a picture

together. "I don't think they want to see me any more,"
Deanna said, and she was still a girl, hardly out of her
twenties.

"Darling, you amuse me," I had to tell her. "You talk
about *they*—the audience—as though they get finished with
people and throw them away as a child discards old toys.
I'll tell you one of the few secrets I've learned from the
theatre. The public is never 'through' with a star. It's
always the star who is through with the public.

"People say there's a new generation of moviegoers and
they don't remember the great stars of last year. Maybe.
But, listen, the thing that made the audience of last year
love you will make the audience of this year love you
because they are average people and, basically, people
don't change much."

It was quite a speech and I meant it. She wasn't sure
then, but I told her that all she had to do was say she
wanted to come back and I would be there to produce
a picture starring Deanna Durbin. Greatness does not fall
from a true star like a cloak. It is in the very marrow and
bones of their being. And Deanna can never lose what
God has given her. One day, I hope, she will call me and
say, quite simply, "Joe, I'm ready." That will be all I need
to know.

20. Music for Millions

It is a curious fact of life in any of the theatre arts that the most difficult hurdle to confront one of its practitioners is success.

Produce a flop, star in an epic that the public stays away from in droves, write a magnificent play which no one appreciates—the problem of your next effort is simple. Comparatively, I mean. But come up with a smash hit and you're in trouble. The bigger the hit, the bigger the trouble. I could name a dozen film makers who are sitting around doing nothing because their last pictures were such big hits that they don't know what to do to follow them.

When *Three Smart Girls* opened not only to vast critical approval but also to the merry tinkle of money at the cashiers' wickets, Koster and I noted some improvement in our immediate situation. I cannot, in all honesty, report that overnight the air cleared. A few people were willing to offer us a "How are you?" on the lot; many more regarded us, as the diplomats say, with the greatest reserve. They seemed to feel that since a million monkeys typing for a million years on a million typewriters could

produce *Hamlet,* even we could come up with a hit. A
fluke. Beginner's luck. Those were some of the things that
were said about our first picture.

We would stand or fall, we realized, on our second.
One Hundred Men and a Girl was the story of the enter-
prising girl whose father is an unemployed musician. The
story itself can only be understood in terms of the mid-
Thirties when this country was still suffering the effects
of the depression and solvent symphony organizations
were few and very far between.

There is no reason again to rehearse all of the objections
we heard from the business side of the organization because of this story, but here are a few. We shouldn't tell
stories about the unemployed; it was too close to home.
And, above all, what's this with a symphony orchestra?
Long-hair music? Did we realize this was box office
murder?

We stuck by our guns and got approval to make the
story we wanted. Then the problem was to persuade
Stokowski. It was not going to be easy, we were told. In
the first place, maybe he wouldn't want to "demean himself"; the highbrow critics always wrote about film music
the way the drama critics had once treated the infant
motion picture, as less than the dust beneath a true artist's
chariot wheels. That Stokowski himself would be difficult,
we were warned.

Stokowski's manager was Michael Myerberg, later to
achieve some fame as the producer of *The Skin of Our
Teeth* and a friend of Tallulah. I found Myerberg to be
a willing accomplice. It must be remembered that up to
this time, with some minor exceptions, symphonic con-

ductors had not figured or played in popular motion pictures.

"That'll be something in your favor," Myerberg said. "He likes to do new things."

I called on Stokowski in a Hollywood apartment he was inhabiting at the time. I was surprised to find him the warmest of men, forbidding when he chose to be, but, as his manager had indicated, a daring man, never satisfied with yesterday's achievement. I told him about all the opposition I had run into in wanting to make a picture involving a whole symphony orchestra. This intrigued him. The orchestra is a living, breathing thing to Stoki, and the idea of projecting it in dramatic terms was not unattractive to him, I could see that.

Still, he wasn't easy to persuade. He did not wear his musical heart on his sleeve. "What kind of music would you want?"

I stumbled and fumbled and cleared my throat. I wanted to disabuse him of any notion he might have that we would employ a Wagnerian Rhine-nymph sheathed in a ton of armor plate to whoop and holler for fifteen minutes. "I don't know, that is, I hope, or rather, maybe you have," I stumbled, "or should have, seen a picture I did called *Three Smart Girls.*"

"Oh, did you do *that?* I loved it. Those charming, sweet girls!"

"It will be that kind of story."

"What kind of music could you let me play?"

"I leave that to you and Koster, with the producer's anxious plea that you remember there is nothing in the

186

world duller on film than a static shot of a bunch of musicians scraping, blowing, or tootling."

"Why do you want to make a picture with such music at all?"

"A personal reason," I confessed. "I used to get annoyed by my European friends. To them America is the installment plan, canned soup, and used car lots. They always act surprised to learn that millions of Americans liked good paintings, good music, and good dancing. They think that because everything is big here it can't be very good. I want to prove that the American people also appreciate quality of the highest sort."

"I'll do it," Stoki said when he heard that. I will say not only did he prove that millions and millions of people could appreciate good symphonic music; he did something more, for me personally, I mean. He proved a musician can be a very creditable actor. I don't mean to imply that he was as relaxed as, say, Spencer Tracy or Bing Crosby, but he was able to play a character called Leopold Stokowski, conductor of the Philadelphia Orchestra, with the greatest dignity, charm, and even authority.

Stoki, I believe, was not entirely unknown to the cinematic art. I think he had been involved in a disaster at Paramount where he conducted the Philadelphia while the camera held on his hands weaving designs in the air. In gorgeous Technicolor, *noch dazu*. It was one of those efforts which pleased no one, not the critics, not the musical highbrows, and certainly not the cash-paying customers.

By involving him in the fabric of the story, we were able to open new careers for any number of the musical great. In the past they had scarcely, if ever, figured in the plot of a picture; writers kept their lines to the strictest few.

Stoki was conscientious both as conductor and actor. Working with our own musical chief, Charles Previn, an unsung genius who handled all these details for me, Stoki used his vast inventive talents with a free hand. He conducted from the recording booth, keeping time for the orchestra and his eyes on the little doo-hickies that mean amperes and decibels and whatnot to the sound-men but which are still a mystery to me. It came out fine so there were no complaints.

As an actor, Stoki was perhaps even more conscientious. On one occasion Bobby Koster asked him to be ready for the next scene which he would be ready to shoot in a half hour or so. "It'll just be a close shot, Stoki," he said. "About from the waist up."

When he was ready to take the scene, Koster could not find the maestro. They sought him in the dressing room, in his quarters on the lot, everywhere, but no Stoki. A brace of assistants was deployed to flush him out of his hiding place. They found Stoki at the studio bootblack parlor having his brogues polished.

Koster—this was our second effort, remember, and we were, as befits newcomers, exceedingly cost-conscious— gently chided the great conductor for the delay. "I wanted to be ready for that shot you told me about, Bobby," Stoki explained.

"But I told you it was going to be a closeup," Bobby reminded him.

"I thought you might change your mind, and if so I wanted to be prepared," Stoki said.

I like that kind of an actor. Ready to the shoes.

I grew to value Stoki as a friend. As the years passed I found him warm, likeable, and anything but arty. He moved into diggings in the Hollywood hills with a predominantly Oriental motif. He liked to greet his friends in a long brocade gown. We ate with our ankles tucked under our shanks, on the floor. When it was time for the next course, Stoki banged a small brass gong. I always half-expected a gaggle of dancing girls to come wreathing out among the dishes, but all it brought forth was a Japanese manservant, dressed inconsistently in a Western coat.

One evening I invited him out to dinner with me. "Let's do whatever you like to do," he said. "Go where you'd like to go."

I plied him with a good dinner and then took him to the jazz joints out on Western Avenue, where the small combos and the clever jazz artists play jive in smoke-filled rooms. Stoki was fascinated. He loved it, not with the condescension and fancy talk about "folk art" that some musical snobs I've met employ when they let popular music in the back door, discreetly. I remember at one joint a jitterbug contest was taking place. We were both fetched by the girl who won. I sent her my card and asked her to get in touch with me at the studio. Gave her a screen test and signed her too, after some minor surgical adjustment to her nose which wasn't just right for pictures.

When we were finished with our pub-crawling, Stoki and I went to his eyrie and there the maestro regaled with me an astonishing collection of jazz music. "I didn't know you collected jazz," I said. I remember what he said that night: "There are only two kinds of music, good and bad. Good jazz, in its own terms, is as valid, as significant as good Wagner or Mozart. Yes, Wagner has written at least one perfectly dreadful overture. There's some Schubert that's never played, deservedly. Some of the Gershwin and Youmans songs are as fine as anything by Wolf or Schumann." He winked at me. "And as for Louie Armstrong, he, what is the word, sends me."

Such a man you must prize, even had he proved to be less of an actor than Lionel Barrymore. Still, I never had cause to be doubtful of his thespian capabilities. Stoki has always been a superb actor, whether on the podium or off. He was able to move into the film medium with a minimum of discomfort and a maximum of ease.

I have, to be candid about it, always been less than surprised at the ease with which the great concert artists have been able to turn into effective film actors. In my view, every virtuoso is an actor. Fiddling, hunched over the keyboard, the musician gives a performance in more ways than one. Perhaps my most pleasant instance is José Iturbi. During the war years I wanted to tell the story of the camp shows that our show people were giving for soldiers, sailors, and marines in their camps. We in Hollywood knew about it, for there was not a morning, noon, or evening that some group of players, great or small, did not leave. *As Thousands Cheer* was the name of my picture. When our Music Department offered me a list of distinguished maestri for consideration, my eye fell on

Iturbi's name. I'd never met him, but the style of his recordings told me he was brilliant, a showman.

A meeting was arranged at Iturbi's home in Beverly Hills. I found a gentleman of medium height, charming, holding a short cigar. I told him about the picture I wanted him to do.

He smiled sadly. "I've had some unfortunate experiences with motion picture producers," he began.

"So have I," I had to admit.

"I've been offered some pictures before," he went on. "I'll tell you how it works, usually. You meet this man and he is in a good mood. Maybe you're at a small party— or at someone's home—no matter. He tells you he's got a grand idea for a picture in which you'd play a part. So he asks you to come to his office to see him. How about meeting at your house? you ask. You've got a busy schedule, you've got to practice so many hours a day. Oh, no, that won't do. You've got to go and see *him*.

"All right. You do. What happens? You're kept waiting in his outer office. 'I'll be with you in a minute, Joe,' he says, if he's really polite and wants to keep it on a slightly formal level. If he doesn't he calls you 'sweetie' or 'kiddie.' So you wait. And wait. You remember how you have had appointments with presidents and prime ministers and, busy as they were, if you were booked to see them at eleven, they saw you at eleven.

"Maybe this guy is keeping you waiting by way of making himself feel important. Your doubts are confirmed when you finally get into the private office. From there on it's a lot of jabber"—and José gives a marvelous imitation of what jabbering sounds like—"and it turns out

191

not only that I wouldn't be interested, but that it was only a vague idea anyway. No, I'm afraid pictures are not for me."

Quite a speech, I thought. I decided not to talk about the other fellows. "Let me tell you about my picture," I insisted.

I told him about camp shows and our entertainers and how much the shows meant to our boys. He was intrigued. The more I told him, the more he was interested.

Finally, he said, wistfully I thought, "You're sure you won't keep me waiting when I come to see you?"

"I promise you. I've got too much respect for José Iturbi as a great artist to do that to him."

He shook his head dubiously. "Still, why should I make a picture?" I'm a pianist. My job is to play the piano.''

"All right. How many records do you sell?" He didn't know. "I'll leave it up to you then," I went on. "I'll make a bet with you that millions of people who would love to hear you but haven't so far will hear you in my picture. I'll also bet that you sell at least twice as many records next year as you did in your best year."

"Taken."

We looked around for something to wager. Our eyes fell on his concert grand. "I'll bet you a new piano," I said.

By the way, there's a lovely Baldwin in my house today. That's Iturbi's choice among pianos, you know.

José was magnificent. There is not a more considerate man in the world of the stage and music. He is a sporting gentleman, without pretension, a man who drives himself rigorously to achieve the kind of music he loves. He is not one of your humorless types, the kind who sniffs disdainfully at anything lighter than a Prelude or Fugue from "The Well-Tempered Clavichord." At the risk of repeating myself, I must tell how George Sidney, my director on that first picture, Roger Edens, our musical director, and I approached José when we wanted him to play a boogie-woogie piano for Judy Garland. We were all very skeptical, afraid he might regard us as tasteless philistines. Still, it was an engaging idea and our boys in the service did like boogie, and with Judy singing, it would be wonderful.

"You'd have to be diplomatic," George said.

"*Very,*" Roger added.

"I'm going to send for José," I said. "Let's see what happens if I'm honest with him. Let me put it up to him, no tricks, no subterfuge."

So José came to see me. (He didn't have to wait; he never has and never will.) I told him how the camp shows were very informal and what we had found the boys liked to hear. And finally I let it out that I would like him and Judy to do a boogie number together.

"When do I start?" he said.

This much you know from earlier pages in this chronicle, but I have not related what I said when he agreed. Surprised, I blurted out: "Don't you object?"

It was his turn to soothe me. "Why should I? It's a camp show. If boogie-woogie makes the boys happy, I'll be glad to play it."

He said it with such simplicity, such lack of affectation, without any of the highbrow airs I have encountered in others, that I couldn't help embracing him. Then I had to reveal to him something that had been troubling me,

because when a man is a friend I cannot hold back anything from him. I go into it now, for I hope to be able
to lay at rest forever an ugly rumor about this most decent
of gentlemen, a rumor which he has himself considered
beneath his dignity for a reply.

"José, sit down," I said. He sat. "I'm going to confess
something to you. When I announced that I was going to
sign you, I had phone calls, letters, and telegrams urging
me not to do so. They said you're a fascist sympathizer.
They also said you're anti-labor. They said a lot of other
things."

"Why did you sign me?" José said.

"For the simple reason that if it was true, I wanted
to convert you. If it wasn't, why should I hurt you?"

He smiled gently. "Let me tell you how this happened,
Joe. During the Spanish Civil War I was asked to give a
concert for the Loyalists. I refused. My family was in
Spain and I did not believe that I should jeopardize their
lives. I refused to play for the Franco side too, but they
did not know about that. I am not a politician and I
don't want my music to be made a part of politics, even
if it's got a seal of correctness and purity on it. For some
reason everybody knew how I refused to play for the
Loyalists; they were never told that I refused to play for
the other side.

"Now, as for being anti-labor—when they wanted to hit
me for refusing to play for the Loyalists, they jumped on
me for walking through a picket line. But they left out
that I was giving a recital for the B'nai Brith in Philadelphia and it was for charity, and if I didn't play they'd

have had to refund all the money and who would have suffered? The charity."

I have to tell this now, though it is sure to embarrass my friend. But my own story would not be complete without this one about a very fine and gallant gentleman.

As an actor, José was a constant delight. The critics found him "charming" and "natural," "at ease before the cameras," and "utterly likable." They said similar things later about Lauritz Melchior. I do not, as I have said, know why the reviewers were so surprised about it. There are plenty of showmen among musicians as there are among actors, writers, and painters, and it should elicit no astonishment that such musicians can hold you in the palm of their hand, whatever they do on stage or screen.

Lauritz Melchior was a pushover when I talked to him about making a picture. "What do you say, Kleinschen?" he asked his charming wife. Her eyes danced, intrigued with the notion. That was all Lauritz needed to know. He does nothing without turning to Kleinschen, it must be recorded.

I have thought a good deal about our relationship. Recently Mr. Bing has pronounced sentence on Melchior and deprived audiences at the Metropolitan Opera House of hearing the greatest Wagnerian tenor of our time. And why? A vaster public than ever attended a séance at Broadway and Thirty-ninth grew to love Lauritz and he grew to love them. Is this Wrong, with an upper-case *W*? A Wagnerian may sing of the Nibelungen or betray King Mark. He may even wax lyrical long enough to sing Walther's Prize Song, which, by the way, Lauritz sang in one of my pictures. But let him sing a ditty by a contemporary American composer, written in the idiom of our time, and he has Betrayed Art, again with capital letters.

Lauritz was not unaware of what he was doing. I was in New York once when he was to sing a Wagnerian role for the two hundredth time, if my memory serves me. *Thrill of a Romance,* the first picture we did together, had opened not long before at the Capitol in New York. Lauritz had told me with some amusement how the stuffier ladies and gentlemen of the Met had gone, almost clandestinely, to the movie house to see "what Hollywood had done to our Lauritz." They had come away utterly confused. They themselves professed to be massively disappointed; but they could not help noting that the audience adored him as a personality and a singer.

Lauritz and Kleinschen were giving a party that evening and they insisted I come. Immediately I arrived, I was aware of a cold front. Most of the guests were from the opera world; Edward Johnson, then general manager of the company, was there. I had no sooner arrived and been introduced than I was cut off, isolated from the main body of the party and assailed by a hard core of musical friends of Lauritz's.

"What are you doing to him?" I was asked in a dozen ways.

Luckily Lauritz was not far from my side. "I'll tell you one thing he's doing," he said jovially. "I made more money from one record of a song in one of his pictures than I made in two years at the Met. But that's not what is important. What counts is that I'm *known.* A taxi driver said to me the other day that he saw my picture at Loew's Lexington. 'I sure like to hear you do an opera one day, Mister Melchior.' That's what Joe's doing for me and for opera in America," Lauritz said, engulfing me in a hug.

Lauritz is far too fine a man ever to have discussed the consequences of his film experience with me. Let it be said that he was the first of the opera old guard to realize there are not two publics, one which goes to the ancient pile on Broadway, and everybody else. Lauritz made it possible for Helen Traubel and Ezio Pinza, among others, to branch out, to bring their magnificent musical gifts to audiences somewhat west and north of the Opera House.

As a producer, necessarily concerned with budgets, there is a further point that I should make. Opera is magnificent; it is a great art form; more power to it. But why should the artists have to subsidize it? The great stars of the world of opera work for a pittance, a sum I would be ashamed to offer a first-class stuntman called on to take an auto off a cliff. The stars do this out of love for music, and at a sacrifice to themselves. If there is éclat to be derived from being billed as a "member of the Metropolitan Opera Company," be assured that many recitalists do quite well without it. Singers like Melchior, Pinza, and Traubel sang for the Met because they loved the company.

It's ridiculous to say it is wrong for them to turn a dollar at the Sands in Las Vegas, or to sing a song in syncopated rhythm in a picture or for a record because the dignity of the Met is involved. If I may be permitted an observation, there is no true artist who does not want to enlarge his audience. You would be surprised at some of the Integrity Boys who have told their managers to come and see me about picture work. I do not blame them for it. It is not true that audiences are fearful monsters demanding that the artist cheapen himself and his art. They are human beings, who love to laugh, to cry, to be moved, and to be gay. Perhaps one day even an opera impresario will understand this, too.

21. *Dietrich Rides Again*

IN 1938 a group of motion picture exhibitors, theatre owners and the like, pooled contributions and took space in the motion picture trade papers to enlighten those of us who made films on the facts of life.

They told us that we, sitting in our expensive offices, knew little of the realities of the motion picture business. There were a number of so-called stars, they said, who literally kept people away from their theatres. We producers thought many of these people important but they were, we were told, "box-office poison." Among the stars they named as "poisonalities" were Joan Crawford, Katharine Hepburn, and Marlene Dietrich.

The years have, of course, proved how absurd these gentlemen were. But it is apparently a lesson that many people have to learn time and time again. Joan Crawford went on to greater artistic and financial successes than she had ever known; Katharine Hepburn has proved one of our most formidable box-office attractions; and Marlene—well, let us talk about Marlene.

Even while I had the Deanna Durbin pictures under way, I wanted to do something different. Universal being a studio with a pronounced partiality for the Western picture, or "hoss-opry," I began playing with the idea of making such a picture myself. Naturally I wished to avoid the conventional Western entirely, in mood, story, and casting. I ran across an old Western starring Tom Mix, *Destry*, which seemed to fill the bill perfectly. Destry was a quiet man, not your typical Western hero hankerin' for a fight, quick on the draw. When my writers Bruce Manning and Felix Jackson got through with him, Destry not only wasn't hankerin', he just *wouldn't* fight.

Then it came to me that Marlene Dietrich ought to be the heroine. I had met her, it will be recalled, under very revealing circumstances in Berlin; at various times, I ran into her briefly at parties here and there. And, to tell the truth, I had followed her career with mounting dismay. Not entirely through her fault, she had become so stylized and rigid that she had achieved a curious lifelessness on the screen. In *The Scarlet Empress* there were so many angles, so many trick shots, so many doodads, ribbons, rosettes around her that she scarcely seemed human at all. A mannequin in a shop window might have posed for this static film.

I knew this wasn't Marlene Dietrich. I said to myself, here is a hero like Destry. His girl won't be the typical simpering Western heroine, suffering silently, entreating her man to take care of himself. First place, she ought to be a girl working in a saloon. Sure of herself. Able to handle rough characters. And, beneath it all, as unpredictable as a cat. Bruce and Felix made a fascinating creature of her. There was a scene in which she would engage in a hair-pulling scene of epic proportions with another girl.

And our hero, far from being tender with her, at one point would empty a water bucket in her face.

I told the powers that be that for the hero I wanted Jimmy Stewart and that the role of the heroine had been written for Marlene Dietrich.

There ensued the usual protestations. A Western hero had to be strong, powerful, with dynamite in his fists, and Jimmy was shy, likable, and apparently soft. And as for Dietrich, hadn't I heard? Did I want to see the grosses on the last picture she had made in England? Didn't I know she was finished, washed up, through? Had I not read the exhibitors' advertisements in the trade papers?

In those years when Hitler was riding high, Marlene, whose contacts in the chancelleries of the world were magnificent, never ceased to help countless people, great and small, talented or not. This story has never been told, and perhaps may never be, for she alone knows all the details; but I knew that Marlene worked ceaselessly to help many people escape to freedom. She did this quietly, without ever calling attention to her actions or herself.

I have always believed Marlene has a quality that makes her unique in all the world. Better men than I have tried to define it, and, I believe, have not done so perfectly. They have commented on her look of cynicism and worldliness, her air of the sinner who finds at the core of her being that she, too, can be touched by love. Jean Cocteau has said: "... her come-hither glances and her feathers hide a shrewd head and a heart of gold." And Ernest Hemingway has put it like this: "Marlene makes her own rules in this life but the standard of conduct and of decency in human relationships that she imposes on herself is no less strict than the original ten."

To me Marlene had always been like this—and something more. I was determined that she play in *Destry Rides Again*. Luckily, the success of the Durbin pictures proved the strongest argument I needed and I was given permission to sign her.

She was on the Riviera when I located her. I put in a transatlantic call to her at once.

"I've got a picture for you, Marlene," I said.

"Why?"

I wasn't sure I'd heard right. "What'd you say?"

"I said, 'Why?' "

"For the simple reason, darling, that I've seen the wonderful work you've done and I know you are great. I'd love to have you in my picture."

"What do you want me to do?"

This was going to be it, I realized. Gone the soft-focus lenses and the aphrodisiacal sets. I coughed slightly. "A Western picture, Marlene."

She laughed delightedly. "You must be crazy."

"Marlene, darling, will you please trust me? I've got a picture that will be wonderful for you. It's a marvelous part, believe me. You'll be great in it."

"Haven't you heard, Joe?" she teased. "I'm box-office poison."

"Marlene, my dear. You'll never be box-office poison. I want you for my picture."

"Well—I'll let you know. I want to think about it."

"You'll call me, then?" She said she would, so we made our farewells.

But she did not call. I waited one day. Two days. Three. At length I got her on the phone again.

"Oh, Joe," she said, "what am I going to do in a Western?"

"Marlene, please trust me. It's *my* first Western too. We're going to have a lot of fun making it, I promise you."

"But I'm washed up. I read that every day."

"Don't you believe it. The American public will line up to see you."

"All right," she said finally, and not too enthusiastically, "I'll come back."

I met her at the Pasadena station when she arrived. The studio sent over one of its publicity people, but there was no one else—no photographers, no reporters. No newspaper knew she was coming, or if they did, they paid no attention.

Marlene threw her head back and laughed when she saw me. "Joe, you're making the biggest mistake of your life. I don't know why I listen to you."

I had come to the station in a big black studio limousine. I opened the rear door for her and got in beside her. We started for the studio. She was telling me about her trip and chiding me for being a foolish man who'd risk a failure out of pure sentimentality. I didn't reply. I took out a sack of Bull Durham and some cigarette papers, blew at one until I had a single paper. Then with one hand, using my teeth to open the neck of the sack, I dropped tobacco onto the paper, wet the length of it, closed the sack and held out the makings to her. "Cigarette?"

"What're you doing?" she asked.

"Showing you the first thing I want you to learn. I want you to be able to take the fixin's and make a smoke for yourself with one hand."

Her smile was like a sunny morning. "You know, this picture might be fun at that." Then her face clouded suddenly. "But I haven't seen the script. If I still don't think it's right for me, may I back out?"

"You may indeed," I assured her.

I got her favorite composer, Frederick Hollander, who had written "Falling in Love Again," which she had sung in *The Blue Angel*, to write another song for her in this picture. With Frank Loesser's lyrics, Marlene made "See What the Boys in the Back Room Will Have" almost as famous as her first song.

You will forgive an unseemly display of immodesty, but I was delighted with *Destry* when we finished shooting it. Jimmy Stewart, in his quiet, competent way, set the pattern for a new kind of Western hero. And Marlene, brawling, exerting her charms among the rough men of the frontier, made you feel for once that not all the saloon girls had kid brothers in Harvard.

When we were finished I took Marlene out to dinner. I felt pretty good, but she was blue. I ordered a bottle of Mercier '28. I held my glass up to her.

"For the first time," she said, "I did a picture without knowing what it was all about. I'm not sure it was the right thing to do."

"It was exactly the right thing, Marlene."

"If anything comes of this," she said, sipping, "then I owe everything to you."

"You owe me nothing. You are the one. The artist has it in him. I'm just the window—that's all the producer ever is."

"No," she insisted. "I'll owe you a part of my life. Joe ... I want to give you something you'll remember," she added quickly, impulsively. "What do you want? Ask anything and it's yours if I can possibly do it."

I had a fork in my hand and I put it against the table and broke it in two. I gave her half of it. "All right," I said. "When I want to take you up on it, I'll send you my half."

"What do you want?"

"I don't know. I need some time to think about it."

The next day I went to a jeweler and had the broken fork copied in something more seemly than restaurant silverplate. When I brought it to Marlene I told her I'd decided what I wanted of her. "You can give me twenty-four hours of your life to do with as I please," I told her.

She put her hand out, smiling. "It's a deal."

Some weeks later I took her to one of Los Angeles' suburbs to see the preview of *Destry Rides Again*. It was the wrong crowd; an audience which had come to see a "woman's picture," a soap-opera kind of thing, found itself looking at our sophisticated—we hoped—Western. All the nuances, the shading that George Marshall, our director, had gotten so well on the film, I thought, were completely lost on the audience. I sat with Marlene and directly behind us two ladies were loud in their comments. "Did you ever see anything so ridiculous?" Or: "Imagine spending good money on something like this." (They had the critical wit of the movie critic of the *New Yorker*.)

Marlene left before the final fadeout. I waited to confer with our executives. They didn't know whether it was good, bad, or indifferent. It wasn't played according to the rules and they didn't know how to react. I went to see Marlene.

"I think you've got a flop, Joe," she said.

"Does our bet still go?"

"Of course," she said. "A bet's a bet, isn't it?"

"That's all I want to know."

Herb Sterne, an assiduous chronicler of the history of the movies, writing in 1941 in *Script* Magazine, has told the whole story from the point of view of an outsider:

Marlene had become known as the Jinx Girl. She had beauty, a reputation, glamour to burn, but Hollywood had forgotten how to market these utterly saleable qualities. Just at the time when Marlene needed a good picture most, she went to England and made *Knight Without Armour,* the poorest picture of all.

On her return to Hollywood she was given what, in certain circles, is known as the brush-off. Her publicist worked hard but no parts were forthcoming. Finally she sailed for France firmly determined to make a picture, a good picture, a box-office picture. Financial difficulties arose; production never started. It seemed as though the miraculous Marlene would be lost to the screen forever. During these dark hours her admirers burned candles, uttered prayers and placed posies at the feet of the Gods of Celluloid.

Joe Pasternak came to the rescue. He recalled the lady from exile, placed her in a boisterous western, *Destry Rides Again. . . .* The film shattered the mold which had long imprisoned the actress and restored some of the vitality and resonance of the star's earlier characterizations. Dietrich rode again on the crest of a money picture.

Marlene and I made three pictures together. As with everything this woman touches, the experience of each was unforgettable. She is the most self-conscious of women and yet, like many artists who know their craft absolutely and are aware every moment of what they are doing, she never tries to give the impression of effortlessness. She knows just how she should be lit and it is not from vanity or know-it-all. Every cameraman who has ever worked with her has had to agree she was quite right. She is always precisely studied; on the stage she always had a full-length mirror or two nearby so she could see just what she was doing and whether or not it was effective. But, believe me, she is not vain. I was not surprised when I read that the lady who has attended her in the powder room of the Colony in New York reports that in twenty years she has never observed Miss Dietrich stop to fuss or make up at the mirror. Marlene is studied where it counts.

Once I asked Marlene what was her favorite picture. *"The Devil Is a Woman,"* she answered. I asked her why. "Because I was most beautiful in that," she said.

She talks about herself as a baseball pitcher or a golfer might. "My control was working," the pitcher might say, and no one would think him vain. "I was driving well and my putting was perfect," many a golfer has said after winning a tournament. Marlene is just as matter-of-fact about her talent.

Frankly and avowedly a glamour girl and a beauty, she lives accordingly. Two or three years ago she was asked by the officers of the Academy to present one of the technical awards at the annual Oscar presentations. Every young star who preceded her came out floating on gossamer tulles and net. Their shoulders were bare and the colors of their gowns were delicate pastels, pink and rose and soft peach. When it came Marlene's turn to walk out, the audience gasped. Marlene wore a long black dress, cut very tight, with a high neckline and sleeves to the wrists. A slash in the skirt permitted her to walk and permitted a glimpse of her magnificent legs. Believe me, she knew what she was doing. And the younger girls couldn't even compete with her.

I think this indicates Marlene's secret. Whatever she does, she does very well. Her cakes and cookies—as I can vouch myself—are magnificent. As a hostess at a dinner party, or your guest, or the lady you are lucky enough to sit next to, she is without a peer: she is witty, attentive, charming, and lovely. When she gives, she gives utterly. Friends claim she "persecutes with kindness." One of my assistant directors, sent home from the set one morning with a high fever, was astonished that evening to wake from his febrile sleeping to find a lady on hands and knees scrubbing his kitchen floor. It was the star of the picture he was working on, Marlene Dietrich, who heard he lived alone, had brought over some clear chicken soup and, finding his kitchen floor could stand a washing, did the job herself.

The last picture we made together was, in many ways, our most interesting. It was called *The Flame of New Orleans* and it remains the only American film to have been directed by René Clair. It will be recalled how much

we who worked in Germany in the first days of the talking pictures owed to this great French director. When
Marlene and I learned that Clair was a refugee from the
Vichy government and that he was actually in America,
we hardly had to exchange a word on the subject.

"What do you say?" I asked Marlene.

"I think it'd be wonderful."

The Flame of New Orleans was not an unqualified
success. I do not think it made the bookkeepers at Universal very happy. The critics were, I thought, unfair to
René. It is my firm conviction that if Clair had made this
same picture in France and it had come over here with
a French soundtrack and the usual subtitles, the critical
ladies and gentlemen would have been talking about
"Gallic wit," "the deft French touch," and "Latin sauci-
ness." As it was, they jumped on us hard for trying to do
something a little different. And—I'm sure unconsciously—
they berated René Clair for making films in this country
instead of France, not realizing that René had come here
in search of that freedom which his pictures have always
sung.

And Marlene? The critics were most cruel to her, chiding her for being mannered again and all the rest of it.
She thought she was spoofing her old self, but apparently
the gentle satire was lost. Marlene didn't mind. It was
the spring of 1941. France, the Low Countries, most of
Europe, had been overrun, and Marlene's heart was not
entirely centered on making motion pictures. She was
thinking about the war and her adopted country's im-
minent part in it. Myself, I was trying to get out of my

contract with Universal, so we did not talk of making any more pictures together.

Marlene spent three solid years during the war entertaining our troops. She was with them in the winter frosts and under the hot sun. She never asked a favor, was willing to do anything that amused the boys. She played a musical saw for them, put on a jeweled sheath over long GI underwear; she bathed out of a helmet like an infantryman, slept on the ground, refused to be evacuated when there was artillery fire around her. During these three years she did not make one picture, and she did not care. It was entirely fitting, I think, for the War Department to give her a Medal of Freedom.

Some years later, Marlene opened in a night club act in Las Vegas. She was breathlessly beautiful, magnificent— pure Dietrich. When I went to her dressing room, she held out her hand to me. "When are you going to collect your bet, Joe?" she greeted me. "I'm not getting any younger, you know."

It was remarkable that she should have remembered at all, but she is that kind of person.

"You'll never be too old, darling," I told her. I wasn't just saying nice things to a great star after a successful opening. Perfection is ageless. And it's a pretty wonderful feeling for a man to know that he owns one day of Marlene Dietrich's life.

22. *Fadeout, Fadein*

"So you're Deanna Durbin's father," Bob Benchley once
said to me. As a matter of fact, I had *him* in to talk about
playing Deanna's father. "You look like her, y' know?"
he added, studying me. "I suppose you had to change your
name for picture purposes, eh?"

I had met Benchley once or twice before, the first time
at one of those fabulous Sunday evenings at the Trocadero
when new, promising acts got a chance to show their stuff
to an audience of picture people. We were standing outside on a windy evening when Benchley emerged, turned
to a gentleman in a uniform covered with braid, and said,
"Get me a taxi, will you?"

The gold-braid studied Benchley. "I'm an admiral," he
said, severely.

"Hm," Bob muttered, "a battleship would do me no
good. Thanks just the same."

I gave Bob a lift that night. A year or two later, the part
came up. I never knew him to say a malicious thing, but
it did occur to me that if I was going to be that closely
identified with Miss Durbin, whether as a joke or not,
there were some matters in which I would have to assume

greater responsibility than I had in the past. Anyway, as a result of Bob's remark, I asked for and received—after the usual legal palaver—my release from Universal. It ended an association of fifteen years. I never regretted the move, for I had no sooner made my decision public than Sam Katz, one of Metro-Goldwyn-Mayer's top executives, got in touch with me and asked me to join his company. Yet in many ways I was saddened at leaving Universal.

Incidentally, Bob was wonderful in *Nice Girl* with Deanna. He set only one condition for accepting the part. "I am not a teetotaler," he told me before he put pen to contract.

"I understand. What of it?"

"I like to have a martini in the late afternoon. It picks me up."

"Why not?"

During shooting I visited him once in his dressing room on the set. Bob poured something from a huge thermos bottle into a small glass. Then he held up the thermos. "This is that martini I told you about," he said.

Another association came to an end shortly before all this. It is difficult to write about the end of a marriage. I am a family man who believes that everything good begins in the home. Yet my relationship with Margaret never seemed to achieve a firm grounding. If there's any point in assessing blame or demerit in such circumstances, I gladly assume it all. We had no children and the parting hurt no one but two adults, one of whom, I knew, richly deserved it.

Though Margaret and I had both known for some time

that our marriage would end, when the time for the divorce came it upset us both. I was shooting *One Hundred Men and a Girl* and I was having story and front-office trouble. The divorce was granted by Judge Charles E. Haas of the Superior Court of the County of Los Angeles. For some curious reason (it was the only pleasure I could derive from the whole unhappy event) the Los Angeles papers, which usually batten on such matters, carried not a word.

That evening, after a long story conference at the studio, Bruce Manning was driving me to my house in Beverly Hills. He kept shifting his eyes from the road to me.

"What's the matter, Joe?" he said.

"Nothing."

He tactfully let the matter drop. He thought I was worrying about the picture.

He pulled up before my house. "Look," he said, with some surprise. "It's dark. Where's Margaret?"

Not even my best friends knew that my marriage had come to an end.

One of the less happy functions that befalls a producer of motion pictures is that of encountering people who come to Hollywood with a vague desire to break into motion pictures. I say these words advisedly because if the persons involved have no talent, it is not easy or pleasant to disabuse them of their hopes and aspirations. You yourself may think you're wrong, and you may be. And even if they have a gift for theatre, a producer knows

213

better than most people how much heartbreak lies on the road to success, and beyond.

All this is said by way of prologue to an event which occurred about two years after I had become a bachelor again. Socially I was at loose ends, the extra man at a party who might or might not show up, depending on the pressure of work.

One Sunday night Billy Wilkerson called me and asked me to join him for dinner at Ciro's, the supper club he had recently opened on the Sunset Strip. He had felt, as he always does in situations like this, that "the town needs such a place."

We sat alone at a ringside table, chewing the cud of what is wrong with the motion picture business and why, the usual subject for large and small talk in Hollywood. The rhumba band played vigorously. I looked up from the table to see a most fetching back view of a girl dancing with smooth grace and ease past my eyes.

"Isn't she lovely?" I asked Billy.

"Who?"

"That girl there. The one with her back to us."

"How can you tell?"

"Well, if her face matches what we can see, she's bound to be the prettiest girl in this room."

The music stopped. She and her partner applauded. I touched Billy's forearm. "What'd I tell you?" She was a lovely girl with a beautifully molded face framed in the long soft bob which was fashionable then. She had long, slender arms, and the smile she gave her partner at the end of the dance was champagne pouring from the bottle.

"I want to meet that girl," I said.

Billy called over his manager.

"You know her?" I asked that gentleman.

"Yes, sir."

"What's her name?"

"Dorothy Darrell."

"What does she do?"

He looked with some embarrassment at his employer, coughed diplomatically, and shrugged.

"Tell him it's all right, Billy," I said. Billy nodded.

"Mr. Wilkerson hired four of them as a dancing team to do a show here, but Mr. Wilkerson changed his mind. They're out of work now."

"Tell the young lady I'd like to meet her. Perhaps she'd like to join us for a moment."

"I'm sure I don't have to tell you to impress on her who's asking her over," Billy reminded the manager.

"Of course not, Mr. Wilkerson."

He returned after a few moments. Alone. "Where's the girl?" Billy asked crisply.

The manager swallowed hard. "She said, sir, if Mr. Pasternak would like to meet her, why didn't he join *her* party at the bar?"

I had to smile, charmed at the girl's independence and spirit. "You tell her," I told the manager, "that I really didn't ask her to join us for any personal reasons, odd as that may sound. I understood she was out of work. If she wants to work, tell her I'm at Universal and I'd be glad to see her at any time."

Some days later Eleanor opened my door and said that there was a Miss Darrell outside who said that I'd told her to come and see me.

215

"That's right," I told her. "Bring her in."

Dorothy came in, even prettier than when I'd first seen her. Some girls are lovely in the soft, flattering glow of a beautifully lit room at midnight, but the real test is how well they do at a quarter to four in the afternoon. I thought my little unemployed dancer qualified admirably.

"You here alone?" I asked her.

"My partner's outside."

I rang for Eleanor. "Let's bring him in. Doesn't he need a job?"

"As a matter of fact, yes. It was his idea that I come and see you."

Eleanor answered the phone. "Hold it, Eleanor," I said, putting my hand over the mouthpiece. "Do you want to be an actress?" I asked my visitor.

"Do you want an honest answer?"

"Let's always have honest answers."

"I don't know. I don't think I care. I have to make a living. It's as simple as that."

"And the man outside. Who is he?"

"My dancing partner."

"Are you in love with him?"

"Why do you ask?"

"Why does any man ask if a girl's in love with someone else?"

"You know how it is with a dancing partner. After rehearsing six hours a day, it's a miracle that you don't strangle him, let alone fall in love with him."

I took my hand from the phone. "Eleanor, send the gentleman in."

He was a nice young man. He told me how the four

216

young people had got together, worked to set up a supper-club act that would be smart and all the rest of it. Their big chance was to be in Hollywood. The fine print in their contract, which of course they hadn't read, said they could be closed out on one day's notice. Wilkerson had thought their act very good but his room needed bigger names and he'd been forced to give them notice.

"I'll do what I can to help the three of you," I told the boy. "I'd like to screen-test Dorothy—if I wouldn't be breaking up the act, that is."

"I'm afraid the act's busted up already," the boy said.

Later that week Dorothy got her screen test. As an actress she was only fair, but her superb good looks persuaded the studio, with no urging on my part, that we ought to put her under contract.

I did not see her, call her, or talk to her until I knew that all the contracts were signed. Then I called her into my office.

"Miss Darrell," I said, "I would like to take you to dinner."

"The plot thickens," said she.

"You do me an injustice."

"You think so?"

"I will excuse it on the basis of your tender years. The fact is that if I want to ask a girl to dinner, I do not always arrange a motion picture contract. Outside of its impracticality from a business point of view, the plain truth of the matter is that I never date actresses."

"Then why do you ask me out?"

"Two reasons. One, I'm lonesome. Two, you're attractive to me. Probably has something to do with fate or interior chemistry. I've felt like that about you from the beginning. And third, today happens to be my birthday."

We had a lovely date. All right, since this is my testimony and I have tried in it to rule out hearsay, let me say, *I* had a lovely date. When I brought Dorothy home, I said to her at the door, "May I see you again?"

"Of course," she said.

"I'd like to go steady with you."

"Maybe," she said distractedly. "But I've got four dates I've got to keep. I never break a promise. After I get through with them, we'll talk about it."

"I'll wait."

The next day she called me. "I didn't break my promises, but I kind of talked myself out of two of those dates I told you about. But I can't get out of the other two."

"I'll still wait," I told her.

The following day she called me again. "I canceled one," she reported, "but I've got to keep the fourth. I hope you don't mind."

"I'm still waiting."

"You're very nice."

"Not always," I assured her. "Only to people I like."

Having spoken of the aspiring actress in Hollywood, let us now consider the producer. There are a number of myths about this profession which may just as well be laid to rest right here. At least one of my best friends has written a novel about a producer, and a good job Richard Brooks did too. There have been others, set in beach houses at Malibu, or in Italy, which described a producer in love as a satyr, a monster, or a liar, or all three.

But what is a producer? He is, take him all in all, a man, shy, insecure, with problems involving falling hair, income taxes, and a growing son. He may well be a Den Father in the Cub Scouts, an insomniac who spends his wakeful nights reading, a charming man whom women will not leave alone, a lover of Dickens, gin rummy, or Scotch-on-rocks.

There are few of the arts and devices, the crafts, the studied silences, the lowered lashes, the frightened glances, which touch him. Love is something that must be planted in Scene 102 where the Girl Meets the Boy, and we'd better be fresh about it because it's been done four thousand different ways. Our producer knows what it is to be laughed at when the wrong thing is said to a girl, not by the fair maiden alone, but by a theatreful of cynics.

So the producer may strike some as being very worldly, one who has lost all sense of magic, or poetry, of wonder, and some of them have, just the way some merchants of grain, dentists, and hod-carriers are rough, nonsensitive creatures. But most of my brother producers are just as foolish, wonderful, intelligent, amiable, and peculiar as any group of creative men you ever ran into. And though they know, or like to think they know, all the answers, they can fall as completely in love as any youngster.

I was in love that way with Dorothy.

Dorothy was understandably confused, as well she might be, for in all the places where young actresses gather, there was one creature everyone was forewarned about: beware the producer who professes love.

Finally, I like to think, Dorothy was persuaded that I spoke truly. There arose a certain problem with me, however. I adore actresses. I love their moods, their inexplicable wildness, their temperaments, the mysteries of their profession that are beyond any male understanding. But I would as soon marry a tigress.

Dorothy avowed that she had no real wish to be an actress.

"I have heard this before also," I assured her. "You'd be surprised at the great actresses who have sworn to me they would rather be milkmaids."

"But I'm different," Dorothy pleaded. "I have a mother to support, as well as myself. That's the only reason I've gone into pictures."

"You just say it. I've also seen your actress who's given up Everything For Love. In a year or two after her marriage she'll be crying into her wineglass about how much she gave up for that dull husband snoring in that chair there. I don't want it to happen to you."

"But I *don't* want to be an actress."

"You'd better be very sure."

"I *am* sure."

All this led to the inevitable misunderstandings. I was leaving Universal at this time. I went to New York for a while. Universal, which is a corporation and has no reason to bother about personal feelings, did not exercise its option for Dorothy's services, a tactless occurrence that an offer at Metro for Dorothy did little to assuage. By the time I got back, the atmosphere between us was as full of heat lightning as a summer night. It all seems rather foolish now, but we decided to end the whole thing. Goodbye. Thanks so much. It was fun while it lasted. If there's anything I can do, please don't hesitate. There won't be. But if. Thanks. Thanks. The end. Good riddance.

I was never more wretched in my life.

Christmas of that year stared me balefully in the face. I had a date for the usual holiday occasions with one of the town's leading glamour girls, one of those dates of convenience that occur so often in the upper echelons of movie society where there are a lot of functions which you simply can't avoid and which you are expected to attend with someone worth an admiring glance or a barbed comment.

I was making my first picture at Metro, *Seven Sisters,* with Kathryn Grayson. The day before New Year's Kathryn asked me what I'd be doing New Year's Eve. I told her I had a date and we were going to a number of places, I supposed.

"If you don't come to my house for a drink, I'll never forgive you."

I said I would.

When I arrived at Kathryn's, the first girl I saw was Dorothy. She was there with a friend of mine, a producer I knew very well. I wanted to turn and go but my date liked Kathryn's party.

For the first time in my life—believe it or not—I started to drink heavily. You've seen that distracted guy in pictures, how he gulps down drink after drink when confronted with a situation he doesn't know how to handle? That was the way I was, the only difference being that I iced my drinks and put a splash of water in them.

Midnight. You took your date and embraced. The auto

horns and sirens sounded over the whole magic city, spread out in myriad lights below us like a fantastic tapestry.

I waited till the lights went on. I walked unsteadily to Dorothy, grabbed her by the arm and pulled her toward the garden. "Come 'ere," I said. "Wanna talk to you."

Her escort came between us, sucking air deep into his chest and flexing the muscles even a producer has. "Maybe *she* doesn't want to talk to *you*," he challenged me.

"Do you?" I asked Dorothy.

She looked from him to me. "I want to talk to him," she said.

I took her hand in mine and led her to the garden. The New Year had begun. From Kathryn's house we could hear the music. At the house next door there was music, too, and a laughing, happy crowd around the pool.

"I want to marry you, Dorothy," I said.

"You've been drinking."

"True. But I've always wanted to marry you." I took her in my arms. "Say yes."

"It'd be unfair if it's because you've been drinking."

"I love you, always have loved you."

"I'll call you tomorrow—at one. If you still want to, I'll marry you, darling. I promise." I blessed the New Year that was beginning so auspiciously.

I was awake hours before noon. The help had the day off and I fussed with the ashtrays, made sure a couple of bottles of wine were being chilled, checked the cigarette boxes, fluffed the cushions on the sofas, checked all the clocks, and waited.

One o'clock. No call. The minutes inched by with maddening slowness. This is absurd, I said to myself. So she's

222

late. Aren't women always late? Oh, well. Why not read the paper and stop looking at the time every three minutes? She'll call. Confidence, man. Think Positively. Of course she's going to call. Why get into an uproar just because a girl's going to be a little late?

The paper was dull, the magazines were dull, there was nothing on the radio worth hearing. And still no call. Two o'clock. Two-thirty. Three.

Well, you might just as well face it. Soft lights and sweet music, my boy, and magnums of champagne and the smell of jasmine in California gardens and this is the dawn of another day and it was all over yesterday, so what the hell? How about a drink, huh?

But champagne doesn't taste the same solo, not that day anyway. I watched it grow flat in the glass. Four o'clock. Stop thinking about the time. It's over, it was over yesterday, it's over today, so forget it and drop it.

The doorbell rang. Good heavens, who wants to see me now? Maybe they'll go away if I don't answer. The doorbell continued ringing. Finally, when I answered, there she stood: Dorothy with a friend, Mary Morrison. "I've been calling you all day," Dorothy said. "Why has your line been busy? Have you had it off the hook so you wouldn't have to talk to me? Don't you want to see me? Mary said there must be something wrong with your phone."

"Want to see you? I've been going crazy waiting for that phone to ring."

Mary it was who went from room to room checking the telephone extensions. Sure enough, she found the instrument in the kitchen off the hook.

"All's well that ends well," said Mary, adding an un-Shakespearean "kids."

Dorothy and I were married in Palm Springs, California, on January 9, 1941, on the lawn of the Racquet Club. The late Johnny Hyde gave the bride away. Jani Szakall was my best man. The marriage followed a little more than a week the events I have just described, so that it will be understood as a somewhat hasty and improvised affair. Johnny saw to the details. There was quite a crowd at the club that week: in the haze of confusion I recall Jack Benny and Mervyn Leroy and George Burns and most of the regulars of the establishment. Johnny found a local judge of the traffic court to do the honors. He was very nervous, poor fellow. I understood just how he felt; my knees were shaking just as vigorously as his. He couldn't get my name right and kept calling me "Packernak," much to Johnny's dismay. The judge lost his voice when he started to join us in marriage and I was afraid he was going to say, "Five days or twenty-five dollars," before he said, "I pronounce you man and wife."

There was never a more beautiful wedding.

23. The Incomparable Judy

I HAD wanted the young lady for my first American picture. When I moved to Metro it was inevitable that our paths would cross. Judy Garland had already won an Academy Award for her lovely performance as Dorothy in *The Wizard of Oz,* but to my surprise I learned she had been following Deanna Durbin's career under my guidance with a lot of interest.

Our first picture was an adaptation of a Booth Tarkington novel, *Presenting Lily Mars.* I found Judy an angel to work with. She is a fast "study"; once she has read her script she'll know every speech and cue in it. Her musical ear and memory is a joy. She can hear a song once, understand it, and be able to record it. Even then—at nineteen—perfection was her goal. If she didn't like what she heard, she insisted on another recording session for a better rendition. A producer worth his pay doesn't mind that, or shouldn't.

It is my theory that there are a few artists who improve as time goes on. They achieve authority and stature, they become surer of the tools of their trade, they master all sorts of professional tricks and devices. But there are others, and Judy Garland is one of these, who are born with what might be called perfect theatrical pitch. Judy was an accomplished artist from the first day I knew her.

A word about her background might help to illustrate this. Judy made her debut when she was thirty months old. Her father owned and managed a little movie house in Grand Rapids, Minnesota. He staged a Christmas program. Judy came out and sang "Jingle Bells." She got seven encores. She's been getting seven encores ever since.

Having paid tribute to an authentic cinema genius, the story of our relationship must now proceed on more painful and human ground. For whenever people work together, when their reactions to each other are conditioned not only by themselves but by others and what other people may or may not say, there are bound to be misunderstandings. The value in setting these matters down here is twofold: it is a true account of theatrical history and it may help indicate the price that genius exacts of a great, irreplaceable star.

There are, I think, three acts to our relationship.

Act I: *Presenting Lily Mars,* a modest story of a small-town girl who makes good on Broadway, is made. There is a minimum of trouble. The picture is small in intention, deliberately so. It is a happy venture.

But before the picture is ready for release, I learn to my astonishment that several people, who call themselves friends of the star, have arranged to see a rough-cut, without my knowledge or consent. If I had known, I would have absolutely and uncompromisingly have forbidden it. No one likes to show a half-done job.

These people saw the picture and ran to Judy with

226

wails of pain and distress, all aimed in my general direction. Very few of us, let alone actresses of nineteen, are granitic enough to stand up under this kind of thing. I don't blame Judy for feeling that perhaps this new producer from a lot that specialized in inexpensive pictures had let her down.

L. B. Mayer called me into his office. With great tact and discretion he let me know that I was no longer at a studio where expense mattered. At M-G-M our aim was to mount a story as perfectly as fallible men could do. Perhaps, he suggested, if I looked at the picture again, I might find I'd like to re-do the finale, stage it as lavishly as I might imagine. It would be quite all right with him.

Well, I had my honest doubts. Lily Mars gets a job in a Broadway show and to plunge her suddenly into a sequence of enormous opulence would, I thought, throw the whole story out of key. But I was new at the studio. I am also never so hard-headed as to insist on my way or no way.

We shot a new finale. Spent a fortune on it.

After that I did not see Judy, except perhaps to nod to her on the lot or in the studio commissary.

Act II. The year is 1949. I have been preparing a musical version of Ernst Lubitsch's comedy *The Shop Around the Corner*. Van Johnson and June Allyson are to appear in it. One afternoon, Ben Thau, one of the studio's most brilliant executives, a man of great taste and discrimination, had lunch with me. There was some bad news. June Allyson would be unavailable for *The Good Old Summer Time,* as we called the musical.

"How would you like to have Judy?" Ben asked me.

"I'd love it," I said. "But in all honesty, I must tell you I don't think Judy likes working with me." I told him what had happened the last time we had made a picture.

Again, let us pause for background. Judy had by then been married twice. An interview she gave to Mary Morris after her first marriage is very revealing:

"I met people, wise and learned, in every professional field and you automatically pick up things from them. So when I was seventeen, eighteen, nineteen—I guess I sometimes seemed older. But underneath I was still pretty young—not so much different from other girls my age.

"... [when I first got married] I found myself in a big house. It was frightening. I didn't know anything about cooking or keeping house. My mother had always been the most wonderful housekeeper, so capable, she never asked me to do anything. That was her job and my job was working at the studio. I concentrated on learning what you have to know in show business—about other things I was very vague and impractical.

"When I was going to be married, all I thought about was what I would wear and how romantic it would be to live with my husband. Naturally I never wasted a moment thinking how I would get the plumbing fixed if anything broke down.

"A couple came to work for us—my mother hired them for me. I wouldn't have known how. We gave parties, everything went all right but I never knew how it got done. That couple treated me like I was nine...."

228

So she had given her whole young life to making pictures, and she found herself confronted, on growing up, with a new world.

Then I met her again, in Mr. Thau's office.

"Benny has told me what you think, Joe," she said. "This is absurd. I love you as a person, think the world of you as a friend. I've seen the pictures you've been making here. I love them all."

"I didn't think you wanted to work with me—after what happened in the last picture."

"Oh, Joe, how could you think such a thing? I thought you didn't like *me*."

"Like you? I'm a shameless fan of yours."

"Why, Joe, I'd love to do the picture with you."

And there we were, working together again. I have said Judy was an accomplished artist from the first. What she had gained in the years since we had worked together was heart, depth. What is that marvelous quality this great artist possesses? Listen to a recording of her voice: she can lift you up, she can take your heart and melt it with a musical phrase. I defy you to hear Judy Garland sing "Over the Rainbow" without choking up or your eyes getting wet.

But her heart was troubled. I don't know why. I can only report what I, as the producer of her picture, observed. One morning, in the midst of shooting our picture, she did not show up for work.

Not showing up for work is quite a serious matter in the making of a motion picture. Shooting schedules are carefully prepared. All sorts of things, running to vast expense, complicated arrangements—this is what a shooting schedule involves.

But, in my view, a great artist is entitled to a lot more latitude than, let us say, a producer. The quality that makes her great makes her feel more deeply. I knew that my star's failure to appear stemmed from no lack of seriousness about her work. I determined to bear with her and trust she would feel my complete belief in her as an actress, a singer, and a woman.

Van Johnson, who co-starred with her, Jani Szakall, who played in the picture, all of us, felt—and you don't often feel this way in Hollywood—that we would accommodate ourselves gladly to work with Judy. There was never a word uttered in recrimination when she was late, didn't show up, or couldn't go on. Those of us who worked with her knew her magical genius and respected it.

I never chided her, either personally or professionally. I left an order with the property man that every day he was to leave one red rose in a small vase in her dressing room with a card reading, "Happy day, Judy," and never to reveal where it came from. The studio executives, and Louis B. Mayer in particular, never once sought to pressure me in any of our shooting difficulties. Mayer was a tower of strength, understanding, patience. He was more than a studio chief. In truth, he was like a father, both to me and Judy.

When the picture was finished—"in the can," as we say —it was released, and was an enormous success. Incidentally, and I take no credit for it, of course, but no Judy

Garland picture has ever lost money. This is a record almost unique in the motion picture business.

Act III: *Summer Stock.* This was a story we did with Judy, Gene Kelly, and Gloria de Haven. Gene had worked with Judy in his first film, *For Me and My Gal.* Judy had been considerate, generous, helpful to the newcomer from the Broadway stage. And Gene Kelly, a man who also knows genius when he is next to it, for he is not untouched with it himself, was more than merely grateful.

It took us six months to make *Summer Stock.* I have no wish to revive what happened. I will only say that six months is a terribly long time. L. B. Mayer was wonderful. He never once talked of our problems in getting the picture completed in terms of blame or dispraise. Whatever help I needed, he gave.

Gene Kelly was a saint. How many days the director, Charles Walter, and the cast and the crew showed up for work at nine (that would be eight o'clock in Makeup) and waited. And waited. And waited. At eleven or twelve, with nothing else to do, the order was given to knock off for the day. Or if we'd start to work, all of us there, ready, anxious to get going, but something would happen— *something*—so you just couldn't work.

Never once did I hear a cross word, a tart comment, a bitter crack, on the part of any member of the crew or the cast. They all understood.

Gene Kelly rates a special word. The world knows, or should know, how generous are the people of the theatre. An actor, if he possibly can, will not turn down a friend. The actor plays benefits by the score, usually on a badly lit stage with an out-of-tune piano. Something in his blood makes him as generously inclined to a friend who needs another kind of help. Gene said: "I'll do anything for this girl, Joe. If I have to come here and sit and wait for a year, I'd do it for her. That's the way I feel about her."

And so, finally, *Summer Stock* was finished. Judy, reading the press stories, written from the outside by people who could not know all that was taking place, felt she had lost touch with the audience. "I don't think they want me any more," she said.

I tried to clear her mind of this utterly irrational notion, without much success, I felt.

When we previewed *Summer Stock* at the Picwood Theatre in West Los Angeles, an upper-middle-class community, there was wild applause when Judy's name flashed on the screen. Was it merely a sentimental gesture toward an artist everyone in the audience had been reading so much about? Did the audience see the obvious technical failings brought on by our long shooting schedule? Among other things, Judy had been having a weight problem and by the time we got around to filming the finale she had slimmed down many pounds from the way she looked at the opening. What about the wisenheimers who'd "heard" (where do people start these things that other people hear?) that the the finale was a sequence cut out of an earlier Garland show—and that the difference in the way she looked proved it? It proved nothing of the kind, I assured them. But would the audience sit back, disbelieving, like someone who knows there's a hole in the magician's table through which the rabbit falls so that they're not even amused at the trick?

When the picture was over there was a thunder of applause. Outside in the lobby people called to Judy, "You were great, Judy!" "Give us more, Judy!" "We love you, Judy!"

Judy saw me. She took my hand. "They want me, Joe," she said, "they really want me!"

They will always want Judy Garland, I am as sure of that today as I was that night.

So ends our Third Act. But I would like the privilege of a friend, an admirer, and a producer of unfortunately only a few of her wonderful pictures to go upstage center and speak a few words of epilogue.

Everybody knows that in the middle of shooting *Annie Get Your Gun* she was replaced. Later she left the studio. I still work for that studio and you may put me down for a special pleader, but I tell you this: the greatness of the people in M-G-M was precisely proved by letting her go. For they know, as I have already told you, that Judy Garland's pictures always make money and they must be, among other things, hard-headed business men, for they have responsibilites to many, many stockholders. But they let Judy go, for they are men first. They loved her and they wanted her to be happy, to be able to go on to bigger, greater things. Things that might mean money, but they did not think of money. They thought of *her*.

And she did go on, and her appeal has become even more universal. Maybe you were lucky enough to see her in personal appearance after she played the Palladium in London? We all bawled, we wept for the joy-and-sadness of life, for the dreams we lost and those that never come true, for the happiness that is always beyond our reach, for the songs that touch the heart and open it like a secret compartment. That is Judy. Wish her well, return her love, all you who cherish talent and genius and a great heart. For myself, I am lucky to have had the privilege of working with her.

24. *Young Actresses: Their Cause and Cure*

IN the Thirties I had bought a house on Beverly Drive, near the Beverly Hills Hotel and the town itself. It was comfortable, roomy, with a good kitchen and a huge garden where I could indulge my whim of serving a delicacy of my own invention called Chicken Pasternak to convivial friends and co-workers. I am, perhaps more than most men, a creature of habit, indolent by nature, disliking change. I hate moving. The sight of a van, axles creaking with the weight of a household in transit, depresses me more than a hearse.

I lived on Beverly Drive as a husband and, for some time, as a bachelor. When Dorothy and I were married, we made it our home. In 1942 my first son Michael was born. I felt that the house for the first time in the years I had known it really became alive. Michael was a beautiful child, rather delicate in appearance, and I indulged him shamelessly. He became my hobby, my toy, my pleasure. I was one of those fathers who love their sons so much that they rush the seasons. When Mike was two I bought him an Erector set complete with a motor that would have taxed the mechanical genius of a senior in college. The gaudier the package, the harder I fell. Word got about, as it always does in the motion picture business, and every holiday we were snowed under by mountains of chemistry sets, construction logs, magic sets, and hobby horses. Thanks to Dorothy's good sense, most of these things were carefully put aside and later dispatched to various children's organizations around town. At first I thought this rather foolish. Why shouldn't my son have all the good things of life? After all, *I* hadn't had them. Why shouldn't he have the things I missed? Why begrudge a child a little fun? And what about me? After a hard, nerve-tearing day at the studio, I liked to come home and play in the nursery with my son for a half-hour or so. True, I had to work the model railroad and Mike appeared to be too small to understand the fun, but still it was *his* set, wasn't it?

It was Dorothy who showed me that spoiling a child is not giving him your love. I think this is the first time I got to know my wife. That is a strange thing to say, isn't it, about the girl to whom you are married, the mother of your son. Let me put it this way. Marriage is an unfolding, a realization, an endless process of discovery. To me it was a pleasant surprise to find that my wife was not only beautiful and charming but that she was a competent, efficient mother.

Somewhat tardily, let me sketch in Dorothy's background. Dorothy Darrell was her stage name; she was born Dorothy Hollenbeck in Athens, New York, an upstate town, shortly after the time I first arrived in this country. She had a hard childhood, both materially and spiritually. Her father and mother separated when she was

236

very young. She was hardly in her teens when she started to earn her own living.

We had in common a childhood with more than its share of hardship. Now that I think about it, it comes to me that one of the things I wanted my love to give my wife was the good things of life. I hardly noticed that they didn't appear to be the end-all of existence to Dorothy.

But when it came to raising our sons—Jeffrey was born in 1945 and Peter came in 1949—she wasn't of a mind to fill in the void of her own childhood by indulging our children, as I was. I tried to back her up; I don't think I always did my duty by her in strictly maintaining that unanimity of authority that the writers on how to raise children tell us is necessary. Again, I offer in extenuation that after a hard day at the studio my sons were my relaxation—even though it was also wonderful to be able to tell the nurse to get them back to their rooms so I could put my feet on a hassock and take a reading of a nice dry martini before dinner.

This is as good a time as any for me to own up to a horrible realization that came to me the other evening. My collaborator on this book, who follows leads with the throaty cries of enthusiasm of a bloodhound, pointed out to me—not without malice, I thought—that I, more than any other film producer now in business, am responsible for what he called "the dreadful invasion of the young on the picture screens during the Thirties." He put it to me this way: Would I let *my* children go into the movies? When I roared disapproval of the very thought, he fixed me with the stern look of the other fellow's lawyer. "What

237

about the young people you've brought into pictures?" he shot at me. "What about them? Why are your children different?"

He had a point, and if at this late date I throw myself on the mercy of the court, I can only offer that the years have made me wiser.

At the beginning, with the success of the first pictures with Deanna Durbin, I was fair game for every moppet and movie mama within hollering distance of an agent or talent scout. That I was younger, that I adored children but was myself childless, certainly didn't make it more difficult for them. Though I have never in my life —well, hardly ever—let sentiment get the better of sound business judgment, I never could turn away a child who wanted to show me how well she could sing or dance. I will not do so even today. I have not lost my enthusiasm for new talent and I will drive a hundred miles in a thick rain if someone whose judgment I respect tells me I may turn up a talent worth finding. But moppets? I think not, thank you.

The big Webster defines *moppet* as "a baby, a darling." I will accept that and add that the word has also come to have a theatrical overtone. I love theatre and I do not use the word *theatrical* with any shade of disapproval. Far from it. But good theatre is always disciplined. And moppets are hardly ever disciplined; their mamas, never.

Here is an excerpt from a letter, milder in tone than some I've received:

... How dare you, of all people, advise me not to encourage my daughter's talents? All her life since she was a baby in the carriage people have been stopping me to tell me they have never seen a more beautiful child. "She ought to be in the movies," they always said. I never asked for a single compliment. Since Joanna-Lou was four years old she has been taking dancing lessons, tap, ballroom and ballet, as well as piano and singing, dramatic coaching and horseback riding. I make all her clothes and people say she is the cutest thing they ever saw. No sacrifice is too great for me to make for her career. No matter what anyone says, I believe in my daughter. You producers think you know it all. You're only interested in names. I believe in my daughter. She's going to be a great star. Frankly when I see some of the so called stars of today . . .

And so on. I get many letters like these.

Once I asked one of these mothers to come in and see me. Something she said got under my skin—maybe that usual dig about not wanting to give a new, undiscovered talent a break.

A few days later the mother walked in, firmly maneuvering her daughter ahead of her. The child was buried in ruffles and curls. Not to be outdone, mama was herself decked out in the identical dress; her hair approximated the color of a sunset. Her child was pathetically underfed, I felt, all bony legs and arms and nervous eyes trained to look to mama for approval or disapproval.

"Thank Mr. Pasternak for seeing us, de-ar," mama said to her charge.

"Thank you," the child said listlessly.

"So you want to be an actress?" I said to the girl.

"Of course she wants to be an actress," mama said.

"She's been studying and practicing for years. Haven't you, darling?"

"Yes," the child said in a small voice.

"She just loves it, Mr. Pasternak. She'd rather play-act than go to school. Wouldn't you, darling?

"Uh-huh," the child said, nodding.

"You should see her dance, Mr. Pasternak." Mama opened her purse. "I've brought some music along in case you'd like to. And her imitation of Lionel Barrymore and James Cagney is so wonderful I swear you'd think you were in the same room with them."

"That won't be necessary," I quickly assured her. "I tell you what I *would* like. May I talk to your daughter alone for a few minutes?"

Mama was nonplussed for a moment but, I suppose, had no choice. "Now be nice to Mr. Pasternak," she told her daughter with eyes that flashed a private threat of dire consequences, a look that was not lost to me.

When we were alone, I opened my desk drawer where I keep hard candies for my young sons when they come to visit me. I gave her a candy and smiled at her.

"You go to school, darling?" I asked her.

"Yes, sir."

"Don't call me *sir*. I'm like your daddy."

"My daddy is back in Milwaukee. When mama wanted me to come here to go into the movies he stayed home."

"Do you want to be an actress?"

"Mama wants me to be an actress."

"And you, darling?"

"I want to do whatever mama wants me to do."

"Do you like to take all those lessons?"

240

She looked at the door, saw it was closed and that she was safe. "I'd rather play," she said.

You will hear it said, sometimes, that movie children regard their work as play, like the trained dogs on the variety stage. I am not at all sure this is often true.

It happens, also, that the only children who ever interested me were naturally gifted. It wasn't enough that they sang like angels (all children do) and that they looked like angels, which is also true of every child; always they also had a special, indefinable, unique linking of talent, charm, and naturalness.

Only children with innate talent should be subjected to a career. If they are lucky—and usually they are not—they have parents who never forget that the child's life and happiness comes first. Don't think that "it all depends on who the parents are," as someone once assured me, meaning that if papa and mama subscribe to *Time* Magazine, don't wear tennis shoes to cocktail parties, and can tell a *coq au vin* from ham hocks and limas, the child's life will be safe. I know better, believe me.

What I watch out for now is: who wants to be the actress, mama or child? In most cases it is the mama. Papa, usually, has been overpowered by his wife, is passive, or has been left behind in Duluth because he wouldn't appreciate the poetry of life in downtown Hollywood, in a small apartment with a pull-down bed.

After years of working with very young players, I must confess I've lost my zest for most of them. The record shows that besides some of the ventures I have already talked about, I made three pictures with Margaret O'Brien. In some people's opinion she is perhaps the most

241

gifted of all the children who ever played before the motion picture cameras, dramatically, that is.

She was certainly a skillful actress. Nor was she limited to portrayals of adorable saccharine youngsters. I am thinking of a film Bobby Koster and I made when we joined forces at Metro once again in 1947. It was called *Unfinished Dance,* and was our version of a little French film *Ballerina,* with Mia Slavenska, which, despite its quality, would never reach the vast audience it deserved. The story centered around a "rat of the ballet," as they call the very young dancers in France, who out of jealousy breaks the leg of the ballerina against whom she has conceived a hate. Miss O'Brien played it to the hilt.

She was an actress, born to the craft. Was she as happy as the poodles in the dog act? Did she prefer play-acting before the camera rather than among the dolls and toys of her own room? I can't answer that, of course. But how do you think I felt when, after every take, I saw her eyes furtively glance over in the direction of her mother or her aunt? If they nodded, she didn't care what the director thought. By the way, little Miss O'Brien was a jewel, an angel. There were only two real problems in making pictures with her. I'll let you guess what they were. Everything else was velvet.

Miss O'Brien was the last of the really very young actresses I had anything to do with. Jane Powell was quite young when I started to work with her but I would be doing a most charming and talented actress a great injustice if I left with you even the slightest impression that I ever thought of her as a moppet. For one thing, Jane was in her teens, gifted and a "natural." She had the the-

atrical gift but she made you believe she was the lovely
girl down the street you mooned about, wanted to meet,
or whom you married when you were young. I will tell
my favorite story about her in a moment or two.

I think another thing I have learned is to look for the
actress who knows where she is going and who wants to
get there and doesn't need a mother's prodding. I have
observed that this stage generally comes in the late teens,
which is young enough; in fact, the older I get, the
younger it seems.

One day I was walking into the commissary on the
M-G-M lot when I pushed the door open, not too hard, I
thought. Yet it swept before it a delicate girl who
sprawled on the floor as if she had been shot out of the
mouth of a cannon. I walked hastily to her, contrite and
full of apologies, and helped her to her feet.

"How stupid of me. I'm terribly sorry."

"That's all right," she said, smiling, dusting herself
off. "I'm not hurt."

But I observed she was rubbing herself tenderly. I kept
muttering apologies.

"I'll survive," she said, smiling at me in a way I found
most fetching. She had an intriguing throaty voice too,
and a brightness and sparkle to her that made me doubly
sorry for being so clumsy. "You're Joe Pasternak," she
said with sudden surprise, "aren't you? I've been meaning
to come and call on you. I'm under contract here."

"That's nice. You must come and see me."

She looked about the commissary. "Would you be having lunch now?" she offered, spacing each word in lady-
like fashion.

"Won't you join me? It's the least I can do for bowling you over like a nine-pin."

That was how I met June Allyson. Needless to say, soon I was as putty in her hands. I was fetched, entranced, charmed. She had the kind of voice that would transport you if she did nothing but read the names of the station stops on the San Joaquin Daylight Limited to San Francisco.

"I'm going to put you in a picture," I said, after lunch.

I could hardly wait to get back to my office to call the writers who were working on *As Thousands Cheer*.

"I have just seen a girl under contract here," I announced like a man who has just turned up a Rubens in a rummage shop. "You've got to work her into the story. She is—well, absolutely fetching."

"Look at him," one scribe said to the other, "that strange look in the eyes."

"Hadn't we better call a doctor?"

"I'm not kidding, gentlemen," I said. "This girl just breathes talent. She'll help the picture."

"What does she look like?"

"She is tiny, charming—"

"I withdraw the question," said the writer. "If she is so fabulous, *I* want to meet her."

"Lunch tomorrow," I said.

The next day, after lunch, they came to my office. "At the risk of seeming sycophantic, I will go on record as agreeing with you about this child," said one.

"I love her," said the other. "If I were not ancient, bitter, and married, I would declare it openly."

After that, my film credits show quite a few pictures

with Miss Allyson. They do not, however, reveal that one day Junie and I were chatting when suddenly she offered:

"Joe, do you remember that first time we met?"

"Do I? Didn't I almost knock out all your teeth or something?"

She laughed unrestrainedly. "You know what?" she said. "It wasn't an accident. I was lying in wait for you. When I saw through the window that you were coming in, I rushed to the door. Frankly, I thought my fall was a little overdone, didn't you?"

"No, dear," I had to admit, "I thought it was superb."

The point is young actresses must not only know what they want and how to get there; they must also work at it with wile, guile, and smile. Most of all, they must be intensely serious and single-minded. June is the most conscientious young actress I ever met. She never "faked," never turned up half-prepared, never thought her innate fetchingness would do just as well as hard preparation. It is my belief that had she decided to be a fashion designer, a department store executive—indeed, even a chemist or an architect, June Allyson would have risen to the top just as she has in pictures. God gave her an acting talent; but she has helped Him considerably with hard work and firm purpose. A lot of people, and not only actresses, might study her example well.

I told you before that I was saving my favorite Jane Powell story. I will tell it now. Not long ago I was called to a meeting in the office of Eddie Mannix, the unheralded executive genius who through all these years has made it possible for M-G-M to keep the leadership in motion picture production and to keep everybody more or less happy. (More, rather than less, believe me.)

There he sat, grim and forbidding as always. Next to him sat the man who represented Jane Powell. Jane turned her head only slightly when I came in, and fixed me in her gaze.

"All right, Janie," said Eddie. "You tell Joe."

Her agent waited for his client to speak.

Jane, whom I admire for her forthrightness as well as her other qualities, needed no prompting. "All right," said she flatly. "I'm tired of it, Joe. I'm plain sick and tired and fed up. I love making pictures with you. I'm grateful to you. But I don't want to do it any more, understand? Not any more."

"Do *what* any more?" I said.

"To you I'm still a little girl," said Jane. "We started to work when I was a child and you refuse to recognize I've grown up. I'm married, I've got children, I'm a woman, it appears, to everybody in the world but to you. What do you say to that?"

Her agent's head kept nodding as she spoke, like one of those Chinese figurines that keep on nodding once you start them moving.

"You know what?" I was nodding my head too. "You're right. You're absolutely and positively and one hundred per cent right."

"She *is?*" said the agent. He was prepared for a hassle and this unexpected turn took him by surprise.

I wasn't trying to duck a fight. I never have in my life and hope I never will. But seeing Jane Powell, with whom I'd worked since she entered her teens, seeing her there before me, I realized I *had* done her an injustice. I had not let her grow up. She was a woman and I still insisted on treating her as a child. I was wrong and I had no alternative but to admit it.

That day I thought we were only talking about Jane. But after a lot of pain and heartache, I was to learn that it wasn't only Jane.

25. "What's a Producer Do?"

ONE day Sam Katz, who was the executive directly in charge of making M-G-M's musical films, asked me to his office. He had a visitor there, an extremely pretty girl with clean, chiseled features and a most winning smile. Since my reading of the sports pages is limited to occasional handicap columns and racing results, the name Esther Williams did not immediately ring a bell. Sam told me that he had seen her swim in a water show of Billy Rose's and had been fetched by her looks, her figure, and her charm. He had brought her to the studio. He proposed to sign her, then to train, groom, and test her. He was convinced that a great and successful career in pictures awaited the young lady.

Miss Williams? She wasn't interested, thank you very much. Sam pleaded, protested, limned a beautiful picture of the prospects that awaited her. Still no soap.

That was when he called me. In the years that followed, Esther and I became close friends and co-workers and it is not easy to separate my feelings and thoughts now from the impression I had of the girl in Sam Katz's office. Sam it is who deserves all credit for literally plucking out of

248

the blue a girl who has become one of the great international motion picture stars of our era. Myself, if I may be permitted an understatement, I liked her looks. I am partial—a study of my leading ladies will show—to what can be called the "American look." Not for me the dark, throaty lovelies living in a world apart, the great unapproachable queens of exotic flavor and style. Even when Dietrich worked for me I threw away her usual props, the soft lighting and silk screens, and put her to working in a frontier saloon. I like a natural beauty and charm, for one thing, mainly, because it doesn't pall or grow tiresome. For another, I've always been of the belief that no one can improve on nature.

I was taken by the Williams girl. "Joe," Sam said, with the same shock in his voice as if she had just turned down a million-dollar inheritance, "this young lady does not want to sign with us."

"Why not?" I asked her.

"I'll give you one reason. I'm a swimmer, not an actress."

"You're young enough to change careers, if you have to, aren't you?"

"I'm doing all right in this one."

"I'm sure you are. Otherwise Mr. Katz here would never have noticed you."

"Well, it's very nice of him, I'm flattered and all that, but—" She shook her head and left the sentence dangling.

"Come on," I insisted, "why don't you tell us the real reason, Miss Williams?"

"I told you, I'm not an actress and I don't think I ever will be."

249

Sam and I couldn't resist glancing at each other. We had discussed this in a general way many times. In the first place, what is an actress? It is a matter of definition. If you meant a girl who could play Shakespeare, Chekhov, Noel Coward, *Peter Pan,* and Rostand's *L'Aiglon* on successive evenings, there would be very few actresses in all the world. If she could play any *one* of these beautifully and convincingly, she might be an actress, albeit with some limitations, which is to say mortal or human. Maybe she wasn't up to Lady Macbeth or Hedda Gabler; she could still be an actress. So there are degrees and degrees.

And then there is the added point: it is a fact that it isn't enough to be "an actress." This is not my doing, the crass commercialism of a producer who admittedly makes a living giving the public what it wants, which means always trying to be one step ahead of it. The plain fact is that this is what the public demands. An actor must also be a personality. Like it or not, theatre depends on audience. Audience means people who will line up to buy tickets, come out in the rain when it's more comfortable to stay home, get excited when the film or the play begins. They do this only for personalities. When the personality is an actor as well? There you have the artistic jackpot: you have Helen Hayes, the Lunts, Spencer Tracy and Humphrey Bogart, Jimmy Stewart, Katharine Cornell, June Allyson and Margaret Sullavan.

But we've got Esther sitting and waiting for my reply. "Even if that were true," I said, "I wouldn't think that's the whole story."

"Who are *you?*" she asked suddenly. So near-sighted that her own hand goes out of focus without her glasses, Esther

250

opened her bag, took out her spectacles, and put them on. (She is one of those girls who, if anything, look even more attractive with glasses.)

"He's Joe Pasternak," Sam explained.

"I didn't get the name when we met," said his visitor. "Sorry." Then she smiled. "I know you, you know. I don't mean at first hand, but I know you just the same."

"How?"

"I went to school with Deanna Durbin. She used to tell me about you whenever I'd see her. Do you really think I ought to do what this foolish man suggests?" I nodded. "Will you kind of watch over me?" I nodded again.

I've been nodding ever since. Always will. For that girl. And yet—such is the irony in show business—it was not I who made Esther's first picture. Credit for bringing her to the screen properly belongs to Jack Cummings who was assigned her first picture and made a star out of her by himself.

Esther is the only actress, or actor, I have met who is capable of following the old injunction everybody offers in the motion picture business and which no one follows: leave your studio problems behind you when you drive out the gate to go home. Her detachment about her work is complete and immense. No critic breaks her heart if he compares her unfavorably with Duse. She does the best she can and succeeds in giving pleasure and joy to millions and millions the world over who find her charm and beauty appealing. I've loved working with her and always will. The only problem is finding new and fresh backgrounds for her stories. I've had her swimming everywhere from Hawaii to Cypress Gardens, Florida, and there's even one in the works now which is to take place in Finland. A wag has suggested a dip through the ice in Little America. It's an idea.

Speaking of Cypress Gardens, I am reminded of my good friend Dick Pope, who runs that fabulous tourist establishment, and something that happened to me there last year that illustrates another facet of a producer's life. Dick puts on a water show at his place that is really a must-see, not only for the intricacies of the aquatic tricks but because of the pretty girls he turns up year after year. Now one of the commodities a producer of musical pictures must have a good supply of is pretty girls, lots of them. Dick knows this and when I stopped by Cypress Gardens last winter he got all his girls together so I might look them over as possibilities for a picture contract. They were charming, lovely, fetching, attractive, but—and this is the side of a producer's life I don't exactly cherish—I had to be frank. Plain-spoken. None of the girls seemed worth the commitment of a contract and all that it involved.

"That's all right," Dick said. "Happens to me all the time. I just thought you'd like to see what we had here."

He took me to his office. On the way in, we passed a girl working busily at the telephone switchboard. I almost walked into a wall, swivel-necking at her. "Who's *she?*" I asked Dick.

"Our telephone operator," said Dick.

"That's the girl I want to sign," I said.

A producer has to find talent in the most unexpected places.

* * *

252

I don't like to give the impression that my career has been a succession of telling, brilliant strokes, each more successful than the last. It would be nice had it been so, but, alas, this is not true. If I've reported that I was immediately enchanted by Esther Williams, truth forces me to relate that I have been no less carried away by a number of other people who I thought had tremendous possibilities and who never amounted to much. I am a man of sudden, passionate enthusiasms. When an artist captures me, I am his slave. I want dancing in the streets, beacons lit on all the high places, and trumpets blaring everywhere. But it has happened that no one else has shared my high feelings. What shall I think of those people whose talent I cherished? I believed in them once, and, truth to tell, I will always believe in them, but in my book the public is the judge. A number of producer friends of mine, in the face of vast public indifference, have insisted on their own judgment against the people's. Darryl Zanuck has his *Wilson;* I have *The Kissing Bandit.*

It isn't always open-and-shut. A producer's problems would be easy indeed if you could enter them on a kind of ledger and add up what is the proper thing to do, and why. Frank Sinatra, for example, had a huge following when he came to Hollywood for R-K-O to make pictures. He made, I think, two. The most kindly thing that can be said of them is that they did not do well.

I wanted him for *Anchors Aweigh.* Frank came surrounded by eight snap-brimmed types, looking like the top echelon in a gangster movie arriving for a conference. "Frank," I told him, "this part I've got in mind for you isn't anything like what you've ever done. The boy is shy, uncertain—your friends here might even consider him a *shnook*. You'd be perfect for it."

The meeting ended abruptly shortly after. A friend in the meeting with me said as they walked out, "This will be the last time you ever see Frank Sinatra without paying for it. Why did you tell him the character is a *shnook*?"

"I thought I might as well be honest," I said. "He'd have read the script anyway."

Frank called the next day and said he'd do *Anchors Aweigh*. It proved to be his first big success in pictures. But I was saying that I have had my share of flops. Frank and I later made the aforesaid *The Kissing Bandit,* a cataclysm that still jolts my blood pressure when I think of the red ink. As I indicated, even today I think it's an amusing picture. But my opinion doesn't matter. The nature of the theatre art is to please the audience, and even if I like *The Kissing Bandit,* it is the public who have to be pleased, and they weren't.

All this is not to say that one must slavishly cater to public whim and fancy. It not only shouldn't be done, it cannot be done. You have to dare, you have to take a chance, do the unexpected. Some years ago I arranged for a screen test of a great and respected lady of the continental light opera stage. When the lights went up in the projection room, I wasn't pleased with the lady, but I couldn't resist blurting out: "Who shot that test? He's terrific—such a sure sense of camera, unobtrusive technique." I never did sign the singer, but George Sidney became one of my favorite directors.

* * *

Sometimes in the privacy of his office, with the door to his outer office closed, the secretaries strictly ordered to hold all calls, a producer falls on his sofa and cannot help remarking on the perversity of the world in which he works. If one of your actresses is a great dramatic star, what does she yearn to do? She wants to do something "light and frothy," wiggle her hips in a musical number, or belt a song clear to the back seats on the second balcony. That she cannot hum a melody or that she lacks any contact with anything "light and frothy" other than a dessert at Romanoff's bothers her not in the slightest. And what has a comedienne on our contract list braced me with most entreatingly? *She* is sick and tired of singing and dancing and doing "light and frothy" things. She wants to know if I will spend half a million for some Frenchman's version of *Electra,* which would be just the part for her, she believes.

Not long ago, striking that pose on the sofa, I gazed at a contract just returned to us by Doris Day's lawyers. It called for us to pay her $200,000 for playing Ruth Etting in a picture of mine, *Love Me or Leave Me.* A few years before I'd heard the girl sing in New York with Les Brown's band and had wanted to sign her for $200 a week. The studio had a rosterful of band thrushes and they said no. It raised no fuss about this sum, however.

But the perversity of our world doesn't end there, not by a long shot. Often, when your picture is under way, you run into other examples of it. After she was signed to do the picture, Doris came to see me. "I can't do this," she said. "It's not my kind of part."

"That's why I've wanted you for it."

255

"But I can't do the things the script says I have to do," she insisted. "It's not me."

"That's right, darling. It's Ruth Etting. Remember that. It's *never* you."

After all, the public has its own problems. All that's on your mind is amusing and entertaining it. My wife Dorothy and I, stopping in Chicago on the way to New York once, saw Danny Thomas working in a night club. He could make you laugh and cry and make you love him and delight in his predicament. He was instantly likable. I believed he could become the nearest thing to a Charlie Chaplin in our time.

I had him come over to the table and told him I wanted him to come to Hollywood. He put his hand over his nose. Danny has a fine, upstanding, honest nose, not a Cyrano nose perhaps, but more than ample.

"No, thanks," he said. "I don't touch this for anyone."

"Who wants you to bob it?" I assured him. "You're no leading man. You're a comedian."

He played two parts for me, both straight character roles. In *Unfinished Dance* Danny played a clockmaker. He was peerless. In *Big City* he played another noncomic role and was equally fine. I felt we were on the way. But his salary was enormous, as it deserved to be for a man much in demand in nightclubs all over the country. The response from the movie public wasn't an instantaneous roar, as it had to be to justify the long-term gamble for the high stakes Danny commanded. That he went on to win that huge following later only proves that while the public is always right, as the old cliché says, it has a deplorable habit of taking its own sweet time going about deciding what is right. Producers and politicians have to suffer this state of affairs together.

A lot of people seem to have only a dim idea of what a producer actually does. "What's a producer do anyway?" I'm often asked. The stock character in cartoons and satires is a gent in a horseblanket of a jacket who wears dark glasses in the office, chases pretty actresses around his desk, and spends his days lousing up scripts which but for his ministrations might have been masterpieces.

I don't know about the other fellows. But this is what *I* do. I'm a kind of super-foreman who makes sure that all the parts are properly machined and finished and that they fit nicely. I don't know how to write a script, score a picture, design costumes, act, direct, light a set, record a song, or apply makeup. But I think I know when all these things are done perfectly. I try to get these things done well.

But this is just the mechanical side of making pictures.

The biggest, and I've come to think the most important, part is an instinct, a feeling, a theatrical hunch that comes alive inside of you. You can't explain it. Gallup polls and exhibitors' reports and mail may help a little, but it isn't all. Besides, they always tell you what the people want *now*—and you're thinking of next year, at the very earliest. So what do you fall back on? Pure, naked instinct. You feel it's right and if you were pressed you really couldn't say why. You just know.

The producer-in-fiction I've already mentioned fascinates me. What I'd like to know is: who makes his pictures

257

for him? Usually he's involved with no less than two women—if he's really talented, the number may go as high as three. He's playing them all off against each other at the same time. Maybe there's a wife in the background, a girl friend of whom he's grown tired, and a new interest who lives on a boat down at Balboa. This fellow for some period of his life has grown aware that something is, as he puts it, "wrong with me," so he is also undergoing "deep analysis," or something, which takes another hour a day, not counting travel time. He may have a son at a military school or a daughter at the Westlake School for Girls whom he sees when the world is too much with him. This also must take a slice of a man's day.

How do *I* spend *my* time? All right, put out your cigarettes and fasten your seat belts and here we go. The day begins at the studio at eight in the morning while the cameraman, director, and crew are setting up for the first shot of the day. This begins somewhere around nine. I am on the set at this unholy hour because I actually like to be there. I function as a sort of unofficial ambassador representing all the parties involved in making the picture, keeping or restoring peace, soothing hurt feelings or bolstering sagging egos. When the director is ready to shoot his first take of the day, I go back to my office. Incidentally, I walk. I always walk. I am known as the Peripatetic Producer. I walk everywhere and M-G-M is a huge lot. I do this to keep in trim.

Anyway, I am back in my office at about nine-thirty. I glance through the trade papers and read Louella Parsons' column conscientiously. I tell you that as a reporter Louella covers her beat as thoroughly as any journalist anywhere in the world, and all credit to her. She is indispensable. Then I go to work on my mail.

This is usually about eight inches high, intriguingly peppered with missives which state about the last picture, "It stunk," or "It was great." What I will never understand is how the same picture which Bosley Crowther and *Life* Magazine loved, so staggered a character in Wichita that she had to write me about its odor. Or vice versa. A lot of mail is very favorable about the pictures the New York critics use for a punching bag.

I call in Eleanor or her assistant—she now has one; the price of success: detail, detail, detail—and I try to answer my mail. Try, I say. I am sure to be reminded by one of the girls that I have an appointment about some picture that's in the works.

Now starts a series of conferences about something the public won't get to see for a year or two. Or maybe it's about a picture that's ready to start shooting in a month. What about this suit the star has to wear? Will M. Dior throw us another New Look before the picture's released so that our girl may look like something outfitted by the Good Will Rummage Shop by the time the picture plays the Capitol? Should we shoot it in Cinemascope, wide screen, high screen, Cinerama, or maybe we shouldn't shoot the thing at all? (There's always one guy who's of that opinion, even though he may not offer it to you personally.)

During all this, you can be sure that a Crisis On the Set has developed. The star's makeup is this or her hair is that, or that big New York actor we brought out to the coast, for a stipend that's more than he usually makes in a year, finds he simply cannot utter a line of dialogue like "Good morning, Miss Jones, how are you?" He keeps saying it, "Good jorning, Miss Bones, cow are you?" For five thousand a week yet. And this is the boy whose agent showed you those great notices he got starring in *Macbeth*. So you drop everything, call for the writer of your picture, and you two go on the set. The line is rewritten half a dozen ways. "How are you, Miss Jones, good morning." This is ridiculous. "Hi, Jonesy, you okay?" Too breezy. "Top o' the morning to you, Miss Jones, and are you well?" Too Irish. Finally, by sheer dint of pooling our collective genius, we make it possible for Mr. Five Thousand a Week to greet Miss Jones and ask after her health.

Back at the office, there is a frantic call. It seems that the action that was shot yesterday was found not to match the sound track and will we have to shoot the sequence again? There's a batch of telephone messages: two agents want to know if you read that script they sent you, half a dozen people you talked to yesterday want to talk to you today, and someone you have to say no to and whom you've been ducking in cowardly fashion because you just wish you could say yes to has called three times.

By now it's time for lunch. What do we talk about in the Executive Dining Room? That's right. Pictures. Why this one is a hit, or that one is playing to rows and rows of empty seats. Sometimes, politics. Back in the relaxed old prewar days we used to talk about women. Now it's usually pictures or politics.

After lunch there is another batch of mail, another sheaf of messages, and a whole roster of interviews. I won't go into detail, lest I overpower you with it, but I'll just say it's like the morning all over again, only more so. And you know what? I wouldn't have it any other way.

Then there is the matter of luck. In show business we are all great believers in luck. Every one of us knows people equally or more gifted than most of the successful persons you could name; but they simply did not make it. Why? We can't explain it either.

Years ago Johnny Hyde and I went to see *Pal Joey* in New York. Johnny wanted me to look at the star of the play. Gene Kelly. Gene was superb, of course, but my eye kept falling on a boy dancing in the chorus who performed with a verve and dash that all but stole every scene he was in.

"Who's that boy?" I asked Johnny. A top-echelon agent, Johnny didn't bother with chorus boys and such, but he too was impressed with the lad.

"You interested in him?"

"Yes, very."

"I'll find out for you."

The next day when I saw Johnny he was grinning from ear to ear. "Remember that kid in the chorus you liked? You weren't the only one who saw him. Warners signed him yesterday."

I shrugged. "Too bad."

Years later I was coming home from a preview of one of my pictures with Johnny. I thought the leading man had turned in a particularly good performance.

"You always did think well of him," Johnny said.

"Did I? Isn't this the first time he's worked for me?"

Then Johnny told me that he was the same fellow I'd

261

seen dancing in a chorus in *Pal Joey* some seven years before. Warners had signed him and dropped him. Metro had put him under contract and I had used him in a picture without even knowing how good I'd once thought him. I'd forgotten his name. I haven't now, though. Van Johnson.

We call it, in the theatre world, "the breaks." It is, I suppose, luck *plus* timing. Bullets Durgom and I, for example, were riding in a taxicab in New York when the cabbie had the radio on. (You're wondering about that monicker "Bullets"? He's not a gangster, and the closest he ever came to a gun was a hitch in the army during the war. He was born George, but with a skull as unhaired as a fishbowl and definitely shaped like the nose of a cartridge, his nickname became inevitable. He's Jackie Gleason's manager now.)

In any case, there we were in this taxi and the radio gave out with a voice I thought impressive. "It's Sinatra," said Bullets. I thought not. So we listened to the announcer who said it was somebody named Damone, of whom neither of us had ever heard.

It happened I was on my way to our New York office. I told someone in the talent department that I'd heard a recording played on the air and I wanted to see the young man. Had a spot for him in a picture. Would you believe it, M-G-M's talent people, who surely know their way around, could not find him? Their contacts had never heard of him. They tried right up till the day I was to return to California. "All right, then, thanks very much and forget it," I said.

A couple of hours before I was to leave, the manager

of our radio station in New York, who'd been after me to come up to the fifteenth floor to look at his operation, found I had nothing to do while waiting for train time. So I said I'd go up and see what a radio station looks like.

The station monitor was playing the song I'd heard in the taxi. "Who's that singing?" I asked, somewhat startled.

"You like him?"

"Do you know who it is? We've been looking for him."

"Sure, I know him. He works here. Wait. I'll call him."

That's how I met Vic Damone and brought him out to the coast.

Suppose, I've often thought, I hadn't gone to the fifteenth floor? Suppose that record wasn't being played when I was there? Suppose Vic hadn't been in the station? Can you wonder why we in show business carry stripes of superstition on our backs as bold as the tiger's?

Nicky Brodszky had spent the prewar and war years in England. He'd written musicals for C. B. Cochran and scores for many British musicals. When the war was over, he was able to get a permit to come to this country. He was in New York. I wanted the studio to let me sign him to write a score for a picture I was doing.

Louis Mayer gently vetoed the idea. "Come now, Joe," he said, "we've got twenty of the best composers in the world under contract to us right now. So he's a good friend of yours from the old country—why do we have to sign him to prove you still love him?"

"All right. But I still think we're losing a good bet. Since Jerry Kern passed away, there's no one who turns out the kind of thing this man does as well, believe me."

263

He winked at me. I knew he was teasing me. "It's wonderful how all you Hungarians stick together."

He walked away from me down the corridor. A few steps away he turned, smiling. "I'm leaving for New York," he said. "Have him see me there."

I called Nicky within the hour. "Mayer'll see you, Nicky. If he likes your stuff he'll let me have you. All I can say is that you'd better put on everything you've got."

One evening, not long after that, the phone rang. It was L.B. "Joe," he said excitedly, "your friend has been playing for us. I thought you'd like to know." Behind Mayer's voice I could hear Nicky's piano. There was also a noise and party-bustle through the wire. It scared me when I thought of Nicky, alone and looking for a job in a new country, being brought into a top-brass party and told to make with the music. The chatter of the guests and Nicky's piano all made me think of him playing in the Café New York in Budapest and I suddenly realized I didn't need to worry about Nicky. Not when a piano and music were involved.

"What did you think of him?" I asked L.B.

"I'll tell you what I thought of him," Mayer replied. "I told you we've got twenty of the best popular composers in the world under contract, didn't I? Well, now we've got twenty-one."

When Dore Schary took over the production reins at M-G-M, I wondered how I would get along with him. I knew him as a brilliant screen writer and an equally able and successful producer. I respected his pictures enormously even when they were not my cup of tea in all

264

respects. He was an exponent of the hard-hitting, true-to-life school. I wondered what he would think of me. "Why?" a friend asked when I confided my misgivings.

"I'll tell you," said I. "He's a realist. I'm a make-believist."

I used to think that one day Dore and I would confront each other like the Irresistible Force and the Immovable Object. On sleepless nights I could see the two distinct philosophies of theatre drawn up in mortal battle-order. On the one side there was arrayed in somber grays and blacks the serious young men who felt the theatre was a reflection of everyday life; on the other side, bright pennons and banners flying in the wind, was *my* army crying, "The theatre is illusion."

It might have made an interesting dramatic situation. But our relationship never developed that way. Dore Schary proved catholic enough as a showman to make pictures that dealt with racial problems as well as student princes who go to Heidelberg. He could embrace subjects as various as Shakespeare, the atom bomb, Ruth Etting, the problems of executive succession in a big corporation, and a Scottish village that re-emerges every century.

Is there really such a conflict in our theatrical philosophies? When I was a boy, driving a wagon downhill, I often put on the brake while I tapped the horse with a switch. Now I've learned that it's possible for a make-believist to learn a little from a realist. And, possibly, even vice versa. At least I like to think so.

26. The Breaking Point

I SHOULD have known, I suppose, gathered some hint....

One evening, after a taxing day at the studio, I arrived home. Dorothy was in the little bar just off the living room. She'd seen the car pull into the garage and had readied a couple of martinis. Dorothy held out my drink and waited till I sipped at it, approved, and fell into a chair.

"Joe," she said suddenly, walking away from me, "let's move out of this house."

She was so earnest that she sounded as though this was a fixed speech she had been preparing all day. "Is this a joke?" I said.

"No. I mean it. Let's move. Right away."

"Why? What's wrong with this house?"

"Don't you know? Can't you tell?"

"Look, darling, I've had a rough day at the studio. For heaven's sake, don't go making any problems for me at home. I can't tell anything. All I know is that you suddenly slug me with a statement that you don't like our house."

266

"I didn't say I don't like it, Joe. I'm just saying we should move."

"Why, for heaven's sake?"

"All right. I've told you before but I guess it's one of those things that you have to keep telling your husband over and over because he doesn't want to remember it. I don't feel this is *my* house. You lived here when you were married before and—take it for what it's worth— I just don't feel it's mine."

I put down my glass and walked to her and took her hands in mine. "What is this, a home-style version of *Rebecca?* It's just a house in Beverly Hills."

"Joe, can't you *see?*"

"You want to do this place over, knock out walls, throw out furniture? Go ahead. I don't mind."

"No matter how many times we'd re-do a room it still wouldn't be our house."

She looked at me hopelessly and ran out of the room. Through the doorway I could see her skirt fly up the steps.

I went behind the bar. There was something left in the shaker so I poured it into my glass. I looked around the pleasant little bar and through the French doors to the garden beyond. "What's wrong with this place?" I muttered aloud. "I never heard such nonsense."

After that I began to notice that Dorothy stayed home less and less. The house seemed to run itself. The couple who worked for us were the same who'd served me during my bachelor days. They came to me for orders. I thought nothing of it, for their problems seemed to me trivial in the extreme and all they ever required was a word this way or that. Since I've always liked food and good cooking, it seemed natural for the cook to discuss the dinner menu with me over my breakfast coffee.

I worked harder than I ever had in my whole life. It was nothing for me to produce five pictures in one year. When you consider the work I have in preparing the scripts, supervising all the details of production, the weeks of shooting each picture (not to mention other future pictures that were concurrently being prepared), you will understand that I was very busy indeed. No one comes to a producer and informs him that he must produce so many pictures a year or else. At least no one ever did to me. I worked hard because my job was my delight. Perhaps, it now occurs to me, my job also became something of an escape.

My arrival home every evening tended to be later and later. There was always a last-minute urgent problem at the studio. I liked to spend an hour before bedtime with the boys, but that could not always be managed. During the war and just after, the film labs couldn't be depended on for prompt delivery of the daily rushes or prints and often this meant staying on in the office after that last-minute call home: "I'll be stuck here a while, dear. You go ahead and have dinner without me."

As I look back on it, this went on for some time. When, after the war, the hectic pace let down, however, it was my turn to be surprised at tardinesses or absences.

"Mrs. Pasternak is out having cocktails with friends," the servant would inform me.

"I see," Dorothy said when I called her on it. "Because my lord and master arrives home for dinner once in a while, I'm supposed to be found waiting with my hands folded on my lap? What was I supposed to be doing when he didn't show up?"

This seemed to me to be unreasonable in the extreme. Here I'd been working, slaving, and for what? For us. Surely no reasonable wife would object to that.

"Oh, what's the use? You always win," Dorothy said.

Another thing: I found myself disliking Dorothy's friends. I don't mean to hurt them and they must understand that the resentment I was directing toward them was quite complicated. Because of my feelings about Dorothy I thought my wife's friends at the best amiable incompetents and at the worst, scoundrels. I didn't like their dogs, their taste in music; I didn't like the way they drank my whiskey, imposed on Dorothy's good nature and generosity. I simply didn't like them.

Dorothy said once to me: "I know what you think of them. Well, I don't care. Frankly, I don't care if they do need my help all the time. I can't tell you how wonderful it is to feel people depend on *me,* and come to *me* for advice on what to do."

I couldn't understand this at all.

I couldn't understand Dorothy.

I certainly couldn't understand myself.

I began to be grateful for the studio and its distractions, for the problems, for the actors' temperaments, for the infinitude of details that pressed for answers, for scripts that had to be read in the evening, for previews and conferences. At least when I was plunged into all this, I could forget.

I am writing now of a time in my life when I seemed helpless to do anything about a marriage that was crumbling about us. Sometimes I simply refused to think about it, as a child does, faced with facts it does not like. At other times I said to myself I was making a mountain out of a molehill such as must exist in every marriage. Does any man really know any woman? For that matter, does any husband know his wife? Dorothy was the woman I loved and yet it often seemed to me that I could not understand her at all, try as I would.

Why were we so often at cross-purposes? Had I come this far only to find that beneath the thin veneer of a man's public life, I had wound up making a failure of my marriage?

Hadn't I done everything any woman could expect of her husband? My wife had economic security. She had lovely children. She had a beautiful house. I saw to it that she had a certain economic independence of her own. What else did any woman dare expect?

The upshot of this, of course, was that whenever anything came between us, my temper grew shorter and sharper.

It seemed to me we were not living one life, as husband and wife are supposed to, but two separate lives. "Isn't that the way you want it?" Dorothy challenged me when I made an issue of it.

"Isn't that the way *I* want it?" I shot back at her. "What right have you to say that?"

It never occurred to me then she really believed what she said.

A whole life exists in the studio. It is a world apart. It contains its own problems, its own compensations. You have scores of warm, personal friends inside its walls whom you never see or talk to on the outside. In the studio dreams are born, realized, or fail; people you have known for years leave it and you never hear from them again. Nor is it a tight little enclave of its own, a kind of corporate ivory tower. Reports on your pictures come in from Pakistan, Indonesia, Germany, and England. You are about to send a company to Italy to shoot a picture. A writer or a star you want is at Antibes—"Eleanor, see if you can get him for me on the phone." A big exhibitor from the Oklahoma-Texas Panhandle area is coming in for a visit; he'll tell you what his people liked or didn't like. A newspaperman from New York or Chicago or London is having lunch with you.

The studio world is self-contained. It even has its own hospital, not to mention a gymnasium, a steam room, and two or three masseurs. Long ago the management put in huge commissaries and dining rooms for sound production reasons.

Dorothy once called me. "Joe, have lunch with me today."

"I'd love to, darling. What time do you want to come out?"

"I don't mean *there*. I mean, come in to Beverly—let's just you and I have lunch quietly."

"Now, really," I protested. "What's wrong with this place? It'd take me an extra hour just to get back and forth and for what, darling? It's only lunch."

"All right, forget about it."

"Now there's no reason to get huffy about it. I told you I want to have lunch with you. But you don't seem to understand that I've got a lot of work to do. Come on out here and have lunch with me at the studio."

"That's not the same, thanks, so goodbye."

We hung up, each convinced the other was unreasonable.

Why didn't I take a vacation from this private, consuming world? Well, of course, if you love your job as I love mine, you do enough moving about in the course of your work not to feel the need for a vacation. A vacation is boring. *Per se,* I mean. Who wants to wake up in the deep Canadian woods, look at the trees, eat, look at the trees again, and watch the glorious sunset? When Dorothy would insist, I would say, "Let's go to Sun Valley. I've got an idea for an Esther Williams picture there." We took such vacations in Florida, in Hawaii, in Europe. I came back bursting with notions for musicals that later became *Duchess of Idaho, On an Island with You, Holiday in Mexico,* and others.

"Why can't we go somewhere and just be *us?*" Dorothy pleaded with me the evening we arrived in Honolulu. A newspaperman had been tipped that we had just checked in and he phoned from downstairs for an interview. I had to say yes.

"Why?" Dorothy insisted. "Couldn't you tell him that you and your wife were on a vacation and you didn't want to talk shop for two brief weeks?"

"In the first place, it's his job. In the second place, he doesn't think he's imposing on me by asking me to talk for a few minutes."

"A few minutes. I'll bet it'll run for two hours. I won't comment that I've heard it all three hundred times and that I'm supposed to sit quietly in a corner and smile gently every now and then when he remembers I'm in the room. Why can't you say to the man that *he* doesn't like to write stories on *his* day off or on *his* vacation, so why should you have to talk shop on yours?"

This got me really annoyed. "I'll tell you why. This happens to be part of my job. So it's inconvenient, so it's a pain in the neck, so I don't like it—what of it? We'd be in trouble if nobody cared about us, can't you see that?"

"I can only see that this was supposed to be a vacation, and it isn't."

I'm afraid I never persuaded Dorothy, and in all honesty I must even today state she never succeeded in convincing me I was not right.

If we went to New York for a week we'd see six plays and if there was anything to see on a Sunday we'd go to that too. The morning the train arrived, we'd go to the hotel. I'd shower, change and then go down to our New York office.

"But Joe, what'll I do by myself?"

"Go shopping, sweetheart. Buy yourself a few things." A kiss on the cheek and I was off.

At the end of the day there would be a few friends in for cocktails, which always ran late. You were so glad to see them that you had forgotten the time. You'd arranged for dinner at seven to allow plenty of time to eat and get to the theatre, but it was seven-thirty before they started to leave and what with the traffic and all, you had to put down the Kreindlers' best food in all of seventeen minutes to make the opening curtain, and you were late anyway

273

because traffic got tied up three blocks deep on Forty-eighth Street.

If you went to the Copa afterward, the acts started playing to you, because, after all, you were a prospective employer of such talent and you were ham enough to love it and to lap it up.

"But it bores me, Joe," Dorothy said.

"Are you kidding?" I said.

"I don't think so," Dorothy replied. "Maybe one day you'll believe me."

Oh, well. It's a foolish, unrealistic notion that a vacation can magically mend a marriage. I began to realize this and, searching desperately for an answer, I told Dorothy perhaps she was right. Why didn't we move? Wasn't this house kind of inadequate at that? Hadn't our family outgrown it?

One day Dorothy announced that she had found the house.

"Good," I said. "Go ahead and buy it."

"Don't you even want to see it?"

"Is it what you want?"

"It's perfect."

"Then let's buy it, darling."

"But, Joe, I want you to look at it. After all, it's supposed to be *our* house."

I did go and see the house after Dorothy made what appeared to me at the time a wholly unreasonable and feminine issue of the matter. I was frightfully involved with my problems at the studio at this time. A new personality, Mario Lanza, became my charge; his rise was so sudden, so fantastic that I had to work harder than ever.

274

At the same time we were having the problems shooting *Summer Stock* which I have described earlier.

Some months later I came home late. The only room we had really furnished in the months since we had moved into the new house was the den. The house was quiet. The children and the servants had gone to bed. I found Dorothy with her legs tucked up in a big chair by the fireplace.

"Joe, can you sit down and talk with me for a minute?" she said in a strange voice.

"Of course."

"It seems to me we've gotten awfully far apart. I'm not happy about it."

"I'm not happy about it either, Dorothy."

"I wish I knew where it's been going wrong. I've tried to think, but honestly I can't. How did I fail you? Why did I fail you?"

"Maybe it isn't your fault. Maybe the trouble is that I've been so busy that I've never stopped to look."

"I know what people say. 'What's *she* got to kick about? She never had anything before. What was she, just a kid dancer he found in Ciro's—hasn't he given her everything in the world?' I've thought about that too. But it won't work, Joe."

"Then what's wrong? Tell me. Let me know."

"If I have to tell it to you, it's no good." Her voice was quiet, controlled. "Can you understand that?"

"I want to be sure of one thing," I said. "Will you answer me very truthfully?"

"Of course."

"Do you love me?"

"Yes, I do," she said simply.

"Do you believe that I love you, Dorothy?"

"I know it."

"All right, darling, that's all I need to go on. I'll work it out. *We'll* work it out." I went over to the chair from which she had not stirred, leaned over and kissed her on the cheek.

"Joe," Dorothy said slowly. "Even so, I want a divorce."

27. The Great Lanza

No one knew what it was all about. The calls had come from L.B.'s office. All the producers, all the executives, and a number of directors were asked to meet on Stage One.

Why Stage One? That was the huge recording stage on the M-G-M lot. No one could figure that out either.

Mr. Mayer was waiting for us when we arrived, but it was his pleasure not to divulge at once the reason for his summons. After a few moments, however, a magnificent singer thundered at us from a battery of speakers. I say *thundered;* the word may not be entirely right. The voice was rich, warm, sensuous, virile, capable of incredible highs and able to go down in register as deep as a baritone's. My spine tingled.

There were three records in all. Then Mr. Mayer stepped before us. "Gentlemen, you've heard the voice," he said. "Now I want you to meet the singer."

A dark- and bushy-haired young man, well-boned, heavy-chested, emerged. He was of medium height, not striking-looking perhaps, but I saw something in his face that was not unattractive. Mayer chatted with him for a moment before a microphone and then thanked him for his trouble.

When we were alone again, Mr. Mayer turned to us and declared that the studio was going to sign this young man to a contract. If any of the producers were interested, he suggested, they might stay on.

I could feel all eyes turn toward me. The explanation is simple enough. Music, opera-style pictures, or operetta —call it what you will—was my forte and naturally a singer such as we'd just heard was considered to be my sort of thing. I felt a sudden loneliness and the usual waves of doubt that hit you when you've got to make a decision all by yourself. The young man appeared to be attractive but, I wondered, had he enough personality to bear the heartless scrutiny of the lens? He was stocky. Always a problem with actors, I thought. And then his voice was an opera voice. Not since Lawrence Tibbett, a whole generation before, had a male opera star made a successful venture in pictures.

He would need grooming, I thought. Polish. Something would have to be done about his hair. But I had caught a glint in his eyes when he talked to Louis Mayer that I liked. And he was manly and strong. All my life I'd wanted to find a voice with a face. Could this be it?

I went up to the boss. "I like him," I said. "I like him very much."

"All right, Joe," he replied. "He's all yours."

Later that afternoon I met Mario Lanza. He was brought to my office by his manager, Sam Weiler. I found Mario to be completely charming. He appeared to be a little overweight but this was no insurmountable problem for us who'd dealt with it with glamour girls and their heroes. Seen across my desk, Mario had a strong face, an easy manner, and striking black eyes.

I told them about my search for a singing voice belonging to a face a camera could focus on unabashedly. I had a feeling this might be it, I said.

"What are we going to do?" Weiler asked.

"Maybe we'll make an opera picture. Don't ask me what an opera picture is. It won't be an opera staged in front of the camera. I don't know whether it'll be an original, or a classic. Maybe we can't even call it opera. Apparently the word is poison, even on Broadway where the audience is supposed to be a lot more worldly. But it's going to be a story with real music."

"Right away?" Mario asked.

I smiled. "Heaven forbid. Nobody knows Mario Lanza. I told you what we were aiming for—some day."

This first meeting of ours took place in 1949. It came shortly after Dorothy and I had returned from what I had said would be a vacation. I'd had a splendid time. I loved all the people I met, the endless meetings with new faces, the interviews, the new and different scenery, stories and people. But when we came home to our house on Beverly Drive, it surprised me to find that the brief change of scenery was over and that Dorothy and I were still in the same sorry situation we had left behind us a short time before. To make an opera picture some day, right now to make an important personality of a young man unknown to movie audiences: these became challenges so compelling that I turned to them because when I was working, the shambles I seemed to be making of my own life hardly seemed to exist.

In the days, weeks, months that followed, Mario and I became very friendly. Not since Deanna Durbin had I had such a feeling of shaping, of creating a new theatrical personality. I told him that I thought it would take perhaps ten pictures to establish him. (I do not believe this overnight star business. Overnight stars too often become overnight has-beens.) The first task would be to find out what Mario Lanza was really like.

In the best meaning of the words, he was a tough guy. Born January 31, 1921, in Philadelphia, he had worked his way through school in a variety of jobs. He was studying voice and working as a piano-mover when he got his first break. The story he told me he later related to Hedda Hopper, who took it down so well that I can do no better than to use his words as she reported them:

> "One day we had to haul a couple of pianos to the Academy of Music. When we entered the building the Boston Symphony Orchestra was rehearsing.
> "As we rolled one of the pianos across the stage I heard my name called, turned around and saw William K. Huff. [Huff was a Philadelphia concert manager whom the lad had once sung for and who had been impressed by his voice.]
> "There I stood with a red kerchief around my neck and my jaw filled with chewing tobacco. 'What are you doing here?' he asked. 'Moving pianos,' I answered. Shaking his head he said, 'With a voice like yours you ought to be ashamed. You should be studying.' 'On what?' I asked. 'My family has no money and somebody's got to work.'
> "Huff took me to a dressing room in which stood

280

an upright piano. I spit the tobacco out of my mouth and began to sing.

"The old man who'd been conducting the orchestra rehearsal entered the dressing room across the hall from us, removed his sweat shirt and began drying himself with a towel. . . . He crossed the hall and came into the room. Still with the towel in his hand, he stood within three feet of me, gazing into my face as I sang.

"When I ended he kissed me on both cheeks and said, 'You will come with me to the Berkshires.' I had no idea what he meant, since I'd never heard of the famous Berkshire Musical Festival at Tanglewood."

The "old man" was the late Sergei Koussevitzky, the peerless maestro of the Boston Symphony.

Koussevitzky said on that occasion, "Here is truly a great voice." On another he said flatly: "There is no question of it. This *is* the greatest natural tenor since Caruso."

It was Koussevitzky who had changed the youth's name. Christened Alfred Arnold Cocozza, he was called Freddie by everyone. The great conductor felt the name would prove a professional liability. They both searched for a new name and decided on the masculine version of his mother's maiden name, Maria Lanza.

I was delighted in learning all I could about my young friend's life. I had private reasons, as I have said, for burying myself in what after all is work for a producer, the creation of a public personality. But there was also a measure of dramatic coincidence between my life and that of the young man's that gave me an added incentive. I felt that in the career of Mario Lanza another typically American story was working out. Do you realize that he was born in Philadelphia just a few short weeks before that same city became my first home in the new world? Like myself, he had come up the hard way. He was a maverick who broke all the rules. Great tenors were not supposed to be self-taught. He learned to sing from listening to Caruso records on the phonograph. He had to work to earn his way, fight his way up from the bottom. He had actually started to study professionally just a year or two before Koussevitzky had heard him when he was nineteen.

Lanza never made a pretense of being a "good boy," or being easy to get along with. He had Dietrich's ability to think outside of himself, with detachment. "Mario, you doll, you sing like a sonofabeeeetch!" he would say after hearing a playback of himself that delighted him. He could be equally rough on himself when he didn't like what he did to a song. Even when he was in the army he'd gone his own way. He didn't like the military life and he didn't care who knew it. Coming after Tanglewood and being with Leonard Bernstein one of the great Koussevitzky's pet protégés, his reaction to the army is entirely understandable. He would have rather sung with the Boston Symphony and who can blame him?

He found himself, at length, singing in the chorus of Moss Hart's Army Air Forces show *Winged Victory*. A small group of people had already been stunned by Corporal Freddie Cocozza's voice, notably his captain, Fred Brisson, the husband of Rosalind Russell, who had been an agent before joining the service of his country. When *Winged Victory* was brought before the cameras, Freddie Cocozza came to Hollywood. One evening a group of the boys were invited to Irene Manning's house. Among the guests were Ida Koverman, for many years Louis B. Mayer's invaluable assistant, and a brilliant judge of talent and personality in her own right, Frank Sinatra, Hedda Hopper, and Walter Pidgeon. "Pidge" played the piano. Freddie sang. He started at eleven. They did not let him go until seven the next morning, and, what is more, his voice held up. If ever a man was born to sing and loved it, this was the man.

As soon as he got out of the army, someone at RCA Victor gave him a $3,000 bonus for signing with them. Victor did not know whether he was ready to record at that time, but they knew that one day he would be a great recording star and they wanted him under contract.

His manager had found him in New York where, armed with Victor's token of confidence in his future, he had gone for study. Weiler financed further study. Then Mario started singing summer concerts with symphony orchestras in the outdoor programs usual during the hot season. When he sang in the Hollywood Bowl, his eminent friends saw to it he got the attention he richly deserved. The audition on M-G-M's Stage One followed, as I remember, almost immediately.

Mario from the beginning was something of a problem to me. There was a wild, unpredictable streak in his nature. But that didn't trouble me too much as a producer. Temperamental displays were not entirely new to me in my career. I tried to be even more tolerant. Just then I was no stranger, either, to emotional problems outside the studio; I couldn't presume to understand myself, so I would not judge Mario Lanza.

I hammered away at getting him physically on the screen. His first screen test proved so shocking that for a day or two there was private talk of forgetting making a picture with him. He was dressed badly—he ran to loose-fitting shirts with long-stemmed collars—and his hair looked like a horsehair mattress that had burst its seams. I insisted we make another test. I begged him to lay off the carbohydrates for a couple of weeks, got the barber to chop his hair with a will, and I had him put into suits that emphasized height rather than width.

He was everything I'd dreamed about. The voice with the face. He was handsome, virile, charming. He looked so great he didn't need a voice. We started to work in earnest. Our first picture was called *That Midnight Kiss*. We had the title and, I think, after we started work on the script, some justification for it was found. The plot? Remember how the piano-mover was discovered by Koussevitzky? We also worked in a love story with Kathryn Grayson and used José Iturbi as a symphony conductor.

Mario was an instant success. Now, it seems to me, the measure of a man is proved by how he stands up under two things: failure and success. Mario had borne up nobly with the former. I would now see how well he would do with success. We had no sooner finished the picture than he was demanding top billing over Miss Grayson. In fact, he said I had promised it to him. Since the business of billing—whose name stands above whose and in what size type, and so on—is a complicated one, hedged about with all sorts of technicalities, legalisms, and contractual obligations, it is a matter I have always steered clear of. The charge was embarrassing, but I let it go, explaining it away as an indiscretion such as one might commit on taking his first drink. And success is a very heady wine, as almost everybody knows.

I assigned Nicky Brodszky to write some songs for Mario, feeling that their musical styles were harmonious. The hunch paid off in Mario's second picture, *The Toast of New Orleans,* in which I carried his development as a screen personality along the next step. Nicky and lyricist Sammy Cahn wrote "Be My Love" for that picture. By the time the picture played the neighborhood houses, the song was one of the most phenomenally successful songs of the postwar period. Mario's *bel-canto* rendition of it was heard on juke-boxes and on disc jockey shows all day long; he was soon to have his own radio show for Coca-Cola and use it as his theme. We were ready, I felt, to make our first essay with the great new film personality in a picture involving opera. We decided to make *The Great Caruso.*

By this time, I was having avoirdupois trouble with Mario. His weight was something to stagger you. He put on fifty pounds as easily and quickly as most people add an ounce or two. He could also take it off when he had a will to. Sometimes I began to believe he was in- and de-flatable, like a balloon. We begged him, played games with him; there was nothing that simply cutting down on the volume of grub wouldn't help. But when Lanza was of a mind to eat, the Secret Service itself couldn't keep this trencherman in bounds. Once, for example, I saw a waiter head for the stage with a mountainously laden tray over one shoulder. "Where you bringing that?" I asked him. He said J. Carroll Naish had ordered lunch in his dressing room. Something made me suspicious. Lanza was then on a no-lunch kick. One meal a day was all he needed, he assured me—a round, substantial dinner, nothing else. He was taking naps during the noon hour break. I followed the waiter. He did in fact go into Carroll Naish's dressing room but when I opened the door, I found my star attacking triple helpings of potato salad, huge slabs of ham, roast beef, generously buttered rye bread, and heaven knows what else.

When *Caruso* came out, Mario was grossing, according to reports, a million dollars a year from films, records, radio, and concerts. *Variety*, that tough-minded almanac of show business, reported on what he did in concert:

LANZA PROVES HOTTEST LONGHAIR DRAW WITH $177,720 GROSS IN 22 CONCERTS

... It was one of the most unusual as well as successful tours since Nelson Eddy's heyday a decade ago. In some instances Lanza's share for an evening hit over $6,000. In Milwaukee it was $6,750; in Omaha, $6,180; in New Orleans, $6,025.

No single concert artist this season has come anywhere near this b.o. record. The tour take has only been matched by such big groups as the Sadler's Wells Ballet and the Royal Philharmonic, or the Toscanini-NBC Symphony tour of a year ago.

The Great Caruso did phenomenal business too. In ten weeks at the Radio City Music Hall, it brought in $1,500,000. One theatre in one city, mind you.

By now Lanza had made it. But I didn't want him set in the public consciousness as an opera star, no matter how great. I wanted him to be taken also as a man. I planned to make *Because You're Mine,* a story about a singer who is drafted into the army, doesn't like it, and finally is a better person for learning to be a human being like everybody else. After that, a romantic period-musical was in the works: *The Student Prince.* Beyond that, still nebulous but gaining shape, was the big opera picture. That was my dream, my ambition. It lay before me like a challenge, a dare.

But Mario, riding high, was writing a new definition of the word *temperament.* I think you would search far and wide in the annals of the theatre and musical world to match the great Lanza in action. Did an assistant director call him before the cameras somewhat too abruptly? "Fire him," Mario demanded. "Mario," I pleaded, "the man's only doing his job. Besides, he's worked for me for twelve years and he's got a wife and children." The great star loved practical jokes, each on a successively more infantile level. He ate mountains of food and berated the cameramen for making him look fat. He was storming proud one moment, contrite as a schoolboy the next. He did; he didn't; he was hot; he was cold. He didn't approve of Doretta Morrow, whom I'd brought from New York to sing with him. Nothing personal. He wanted to make the picture with Lana Turner. But the part called for a singer, I assured him. No matter. He still didn't want to do the picture. Then next day he thought Doretta was just fine. I wondered if even back in the wonderfully crazy days of Swanson and Negri a player with but three pictures to his credit could throw such thunderbolts from on high.

I tried every trick of appealing to Mario. "I gotta talk

287

to that boy for you, Joe," Jimmy Durante offered. "Him and me, we're Eyetalians. He'll listen to me." If Lanza did listen to one of the sweetest men in show business, he gave me no sign. Lillian Burns, who is God's gift to new talent, and whom Mario had often generously (and deservedly) praised to me, saying he owed her more than anyone realized, did her best. To little avail.

Finally—after midnight meetings, tense conferences, agreements, disagreements, more meetings and still more meetings—Mario decided to do *Because You're Mine.* But he had put on about fifty pounds, I'd guess, and we had to postpone shooting for six weeks.

He did reduce. He looked better and sang better than ever in his life. *Because You're Mine* was chosen for the Royal Command Performance. Mario was full of assurances that he had wronged me grievously and had learned to trust in my judgment. What was to be our next picture? *The Student Prince?* Great. He went to work at once recording his songs.

On the first day's shooting we were doing one of those scenes that called for a huge number of extras. Where was Mario? No one knew. At the end of the day, he was found. He was sorry, he was contrite. Tomorrow he'd show up for sure. Next day, no Lanza. Again: sorry. Is anything wrong, son? No, no, I'm all right. Is it anything we did that's bothering you? Oh, no, no.

This went on for days. Even his agent, Lew Wasserman, a top-chop character, couldn't get to talk to *this* client. The studio was actually well over a million dollars in the hole, representing money paid out, not mere bookkeeper's charges, when the storm broke. After Mario had broken

288

written engagements, the picture was abandoned and the studio sued Lanza for its costs and damages.

The incident was in many ways the most upsetting I had ever known. I had been—as this record shows—harsh with Mario, but always *con amore*, with love, as a father is harsh to a son whose inner fineness he will never doubt. To the end I thought well of him. I would always think of him as a friend, even though his stubborn refusal to work in a picture in which I was so deeply committed seemed to me to be unfair, to say the least. It wasn't easy to give up my dream of an opera picture. A venture into the cinematic unknown such as I envisaged required a lucky meeting in time, space, and spirit. With Lanza I had felt a beginning was possible. He was the foundation stone. I wished him well, as I say. I wrote the unhappy ending of our relationship down to one of those things: the unfortunate circumstances that so often dog our endeavors in show business.

But then, one night, it came to me:

Why had I been patient with Mario Lanza, understanding, always ready to justify, forgive and forget? Inexplicable restlessness and moods, irrational pets and peeves, misconduct that might have fetched a lesser personage a private or official cuffing—I'd been the first to cover up, straighten out and to sympathize, the first to make whatever personal adjustment had to be made. Why? What had made me do all this for *him*?

Why hadn't I been able to do a tenth as much for a wife, whom I loved and who, I knew, loved me? Was my marriage, was my life with Dorothy and my children, less important to me?

By God, I said one sleepless night, standing before an open window in the new house from which Dorothy had moved a few weeks before, if I can do all this for one of my actors, I can do more for my wife. Otherwise, no matter what, even if you make pictures that gross in the fabulous millions, you will know in your own heart that you have wound up a failure. I remember spinning the cigarette I was smoking out the window. Suddenly it all came together: my public and my private life and everything I had ever learned in my beloved country where there was no such word as *failure*. I went to bed and slept well the rest of that night.

28. Reunion in Hollywood

DOROTHY was living at the Bel-Air Hotel, so close to our home that I could easily walk there. We dined together often. We talked formally, politely, without bitterness or recrimination. We knew that soon we would have to take a fateful leap into the unknown, and each of us drew back from the moment of decision.

It came to me that this arrangement, living apart from each other yet so close that we saw each other almost every day, proved nothing. Even after the lawyers had sat down with us in the den of our home and had gone through all the dismal details which a divorce involves, Dorothy and I went right on seeing each other as if the whole matter were out of our hands.

Maybe I am slow to make up my mind, but once I decide something's right, there is no stopping me. "Dorothy," I told her one evening, "why don't you get away from this place?"

"Why do you think I ought to go?"

"I've tried to understand you, darling. Believe that. I've tried to figure out where and why I failed you, which I'm not sure of. I've even tried to convince myself that

I *have* failed you. About all I can figure is that after almost ten years of marriage, you're just plain restless and bored. Out there—New York, Paris, London—things look glamorous and exciting. Here they're—well, I don't have to tell you what they are."

"I ran into a friend I used to know when I first came to town," Dorothy said softly. "I told her we're getting a divorce. She asked me why. I couldn't tell her why. 'Don't you have children?' she asked me. I told her I had three fine boys. 'Does your husband love you?' she asked me later. I told her I thought you did. 'Then what's the matter, girl?' she said. 'What's the matter, girl? Grow up.' "

"Well?" There was nothing I could, or wanted to, say.

"All right, Joe. I'll go to New York." She looked at me curiously and added: "Unless you think I should come home?"

"Is there any doubt in your mind?"

"I'm not sure."

"Then go to New York. Maybe I could talk you into coming home. What good would it do? A year later you could talk yourself right out again. It's no good coming back unless you feel it's what you want to do more than anything in the world."

"Suppose I don't come back?"

"Suppose I'm not here when—or if—you do come back?"

Dorothy left for New York within the week. I thought of our last meeting many times. Had I been foolish? Had I shown weakness or strength? Even that I didn't know, I couldn't be sure of.

Children are amazing. You will forgive, I hope, this fatuous remark. The boys had always been devoted to their mother, but when they were left alone, they acted as though Dorothy had not even left home. She telephoned them often, sometimes every day, and I know how deeply these calls affected her because frequently when I took the phone after the boys had talked to her, Dorothy was weeping.

When I talked to her I had the feeling that the vast distance between us, from Atlantic to Pacific, was nothing. I felt I could easily reach out, touch her, and bring her home. But I didn't want to do that. This was a decision, I felt, she would have to make for herself.

I knew what she was doing in New York, whom she was seeing. The show world, when you come right down to it, is a very small one, much less populous than a town in Vermont. We have more reporters per square acre than any other group in the world. So I had only to pick up the papers to know the names of the people she was seeing or dining with. We were by now properly divorced, pending only the completion of the one-year interlocutory period.

At this point, I think, it is only fair for me to express my gratitude to at least one individual who did as much as anyone I can think of to bring us together again. The columnists whose business it is to report on the people of the show world are often accused of creating the very troubles and conflicts they tell the world about. I am not so sure about this. I do know that even the happily anonymous among us do the same things, foolish and otherwise, as those whose "names make news." In any event, it was Walter Winchell, who has a reputation for being cold and hard-hitting, who showed that beneath that tough reporter's exterior beats the heart of a family man and a true friend. Walter called me often; I in turn called him whenever I wanted to know of Dorothy's doings. He kept me accurately and discreetly informed, always assuring me that despite everything, if I kept the faith, Dorothy and I would get back together again. I found this difficult to believe.

Then Dorothy, after talking to the boys one evening, told me she was going to Europe. "Do you think I ought to go?" she asked me. I had the feeling she needed help.

"Me? I think you ought to come home."

"For the children's sake?"

"First, for your sake, darling. Then for my sake. Then for our sake. And finally for the children's sake. Don't worry about the children—they adjust better than we do."

But I could tell that Dorothy had still not made up her mind about coming home for good, so I said: "I'd go to Europe until I was very sure, darling."

So she went to Europe.

> Plaza-Athenée Hotel
> Paris

Dear Joe:

... It's raining in Paris. It rained in London when I was there. I understand it's also raining in Rome but I don't care enough to go and find out for myself. Paris in the rain has a gray loveliness all its own, but not when you're alone. The people here look, act, talk, and behave exactly like the people in London, New York. If I close my eyes I could believe I was in Scandia, the Polo Lounge of the Beverly Hills, the Sands in Las Vegas, or the St. Regis or El Morocco. We are all trying so pathetically to fill in the empty spaces with dinner parties and idle chatter and more dinner parties. There isn't one of them who won't cry on your shoulder at the drop of a champagne glass. Everybody is so lonely. The whole purpose of everything is to keep from being alone for one minute.

Yet I don't want you to think it's always like this. I've had fun. Some of the people are stimulating; I've found something I never had before—maybe it's a kind of insight into myself. Still—I'm lonely.

I don't know why I'm telling you all this. Our interlocutory period is about over and I must stop thinking we're still married. When you get this I'll be back in New York...

I looked at the calendar on my desk. Only a few short weeks remained for what was left of our marriage. If there was no reconciliation before the end of the interlocutory period, our divorce would automatically be final. I got up, ran to the outer office, told the girls I was going to Las Vegas for the week end, and took a cab outside the building. I ordered the driver to go to the airport, where I took the first plane to New York.

I had made up my mind. It was all very well and good and doubtless exceedingly shrewd of me to insist that Dorothy know precisely what she wanted. But which of us does know? Did I? Oh, it would have been lovely if she had come back on her own, but maybe what she was waiting for was precisely a word from me?

It was mid-afternoon when I got to Dorothy's Manhattan apartment. I walked around the block several times so I'd feel right before I went in, neither humble about what had happened, or arrogant. Finally I strode into the foyer, into the elevator, and stood before Dorothy's door.

I rang the bell. There was no answer. I listened carefully. No one stirred within. I rang again. Still no answer. I rang again.

Maybe it was better this way, I thought. I was still tense and I was afraid what I would say if Dorothy said she didn't want to come home. I went out into the street and walked over toward the West Side, not particularly aware of what I was doing. I wanted to kill an hour or two and then go back when Dorothy had returned from whatever she was doing.

There was a big line down Fiftieth Street. I looked up and saw one of my pictures, *Easy To Love,* with Esther Williams, was playing. I stood in line with the others, one of them, grateful for an hour or two of being lifted out of myself, for a spell of forgetting.

When I got out of the Music Hall, the hour was just right. Dorothy would be home, dressing to go out to dinner. I walked quickly to her place again. Once more I stood before her door. I rang the bell. No answer. I rang it again and again. I pounded on the door. No answer.

I was pretty desperate when I hit that street again. Once again I started to walk, uptown this time, toward Yorkville. On one of the sidestreets a red neon sign kept blinking at me: *Café Hungaria.* I stopped outside for a moment. It didn't look like much of a place but through the window I could see a violinist and a cymbalom-player. Well, I'd go in until later in the evening, when I'd try Dorothy's bell again.

I no sooner stepped in the door when I heard my name ring across the restaurant. "Mr. Pasternak! Joe Pasternak! What an honor! How did you know where to find me?"

This was all in Hungarian, of course, and, truth to tell, while the man's face looked familiar, I wasn't certain from where and how I knew him. He spared me the embarrassment. "I'm Sam Reischman, from Budapest, Mr. Pasternak. You don't remember me, but I worked for you."

"I remember you now, Sam," I said.

After that the place was mine. The musicians played for me; the whole kitchen staff came out to shake my hand. Many of them were refugees from Hungary now and a few of them shared wine with me and we talked of the old days in Budapest and the good times we had all had. It was all right until they kept nudging me and telling one another what a success I was, a producer of motion pictures in Hollywood, with a beautiful wife and children—they knew all about me from the motion picture columns, all, that is, except that in a few days my divorce would be final and that I was miserable because I had come all this way only to find Dorothy out.

But late, very late, I bade them all goodbye and walked to Dorothy's apartment. It was now, I said to myself, the hour when she'd be home, when there'd be no place to be *but* home. I rang the bell. No answer. I pounded on the door. I was sure now she'd been home all the time and didn't want to talk to me.

I don't know how long this went on. I stopped when a neighbor opened his door. "If you don't go away, I'm going to call the police," he said.

At a cabstand I found a cab. "Take me to La Guardia."

Dawn streaked the sky as we flew West. When I got back home, I let myself in the front door and was wearily mounting the stairs to my bedroom when I heard music from the den, the door to which is just below the stairs. I stopped, descended the stairs, and walked slowly to the door. When I pushed it open, I saw Dorothy sitting in her favorite chair.

"Hello, darling," she said.

"Hello, darling," I said.

And that's all there was to it.

29. *Easy the Hard Way*

RIGHT here, if I could work a miracle, music would come swelling at you right out of the printed page. Large, round melodious chords, I think, something to lift the heart. That is the way I like to end a story; as you now see, it is the only way that comes naturally to me as well. I have never really forgotten what my old teacher Schwarz told me.

Once when I was producing pictures in Hungary I finally succeeded in persuading Schwarz, whom I always saw when I went home to see my father in his village, to come with me for a visit to Budapest. "What will your fine city friends think of a shabby old teacher?" he said without a trace of self-pity. "I wonder what I'd look like to them? I've lived so long in the country I must look like a peasant."

I would not listen to his protests and made him come to Budapest with me. I put him up in the Royale in a sitting room–bedroom suite facing the front. I brought him to the studio where I introduced him to the stars and the composers and the writers. "Next to my father," I told everybody, "this man is responsible for what I've been able to do." At first Schwarz was shy with us because he didn't think his clothes were cut properly, and they weren't. But since my friends always went on the basis that what any one of us had belonged to all of us, they took the old teacher to their hearts too. In a few days Schwarz drank with them, dined with them, and spent the nights making the rounds of the gypsy restaurants with them. He bought a blue suit and a pearl-gray hat and within the month the restaurant captains and the waiters were bowing and scraping to him and calling him "Professor."

Then one day Schwarz came to me and said he was going back to Szilagy-Somlyo.

"You don't have to go yet," I told him. "Stay a while."

Schwarz shook his head slightly. "I have heard the music again, Joe," he said, "the music I heard when I was a young man. Now I would like to go home and remember it. For me remembering is as good as hearing."

I haven't come to that stage of life yet, although now that I have put it all down, it comes to me that what my father taught me is true, as true as what I learned from Schwarz. There is nothing so wrong with people, or, to be more specific, with any one of us that love won't cure. There is music everywhere in life and there is love, but you have to learn how to hear the former and to feel the latter.

I don't propose to stop proving it. I don't want to go long-hair on you, but the world of which I am a part, the world of the movies, has had a tremendous impact on the culture of our time. Perhaps at times it has had its undesirable effects, but on the whole I like to think it's done more good than many people give us credit for. People all over the world have learned from it that, really, all things are possible. If the young people can't get Stokowski or Iturbi to conduct their orchestras and get them out of the hole, they can get someone else. And sometimes in trying they find they don't even need the great man. They find they can do it all by themselves.

When we began, I promised you a story with a happy ending. Actually, dramatically, there is no such thing as a happy ending, for a happy story goes on and on. In a tragedy like *Hamlet* the stage is littered with corpses and that of course is the end of it. In my stories everybody is always around for another day, and my life is not over yet. But this I do know: I always preferred the comic mask to the tragic and always will.

Even if I didn't, however, I am not permitted to take myself too seriously. The plain fact is my sons deal more severely with me than any critic. "Daddy," Michael said to me the other day, "when are you going to make a *good* picture?" "Yes," Jeffrey added instantly, "A *real* picture with cowboys and Indians and stuff?"

It was Peter, the youngest of the three, who rose to my defense. "Ah, don't talk like that about daddy," he protested. "He's *trying*. Aren't you, daddy?"

Yes, boys, I'm still trying.